Beginning Game AI with Unity

Programming Artificial Intelligence with C#

Sebastiano M. Cossu

Apress®

Beginning Game AI with Unity

Sebastiano M. Cossu
LONDON, UK

ISBN-13 (pbk): 978-1-4842-6354-9   ISBN-13 (electronic): 978-1-4842-6355-6
https://doi.org/10.1007/978-1-4842-6355-6

Managing Director, Apress Media LLC: Welmoed Spahr
Acquisitions Editor: Spandana Chatterjee
Development Editor: Laura Berendson
Coordinating Editor: Divya Modi

Cover designed by eStudioCalamar

Cover image designed by Pixabay

Distributed to the book trade worldwide by Springer Science+Business Media New York, 1 New York Plaza, Suite 4600, New York, NY 10004-1562, USA. Phone 1-800-SPRINGER, fax (201) 348-4505, e-mail orders-ny@springer-sbm.com, or visit www.springeronline.com. Apress Media, LLC is a California LLC and the sole member (owner) is Springer Science + Business Media Finance Inc (SSBM Finance Inc). SSBM Finance Inc is a **Delaware** corporation.

For information on translations, please e-mail booktranslations@springernature.com; for reprint, paperback, or audio rights, please e-mail bookpermissions@springernature.com.

Apress titles may be purchased in bulk for academic, corporate, or promotional use. eBook versions and licenses are also available for most titles. For more information, reference our Print and eBook Bulk Sales web page at http://www.apress.com/bulk-sales.

Any source code or other supplementary material referenced by the author in this book is available to readers on GitHub via the book's product page, located at www.apress.com/978-1-4842-6354-9. For more detailed information, please visit http://www.apress.com/source-code.

Printed on acid-free paper

To the victims of COVID-19

Table of Contents

About the Author

Sebastiano Cossu is a software engineer and game developer. He studied Computer Science at the University of Rome "La Sapienza." He is currently working as a Game Developer at Feral Interactive Ltd. in London. He wrote the Apress book *Game Development with GameMaker Studio 2*.

About the Technical Reviewer

An immersive technology enthusiast, Mr Abhiram A is a Unity3D Ambassador for Unity India and is the cofounder of Odyn Reality, an XR Tech startup. He doubles as Technical Officer – XR at Kerala Startup Mission and XR Coach for SV.CO Facebook School of Innovation. He was also part of Future Technologies Lab, Kochi, as a Research Fellow in VR. He is a Udacity VR Nanodegree graduate and a Unity Certified Developer .

Acknowledgments

I wrote this book in a very strange time in history: a new unknown virus spread and changed our lives forever – things that I only saw in video games until this moment.

It was a year full of chaos, fear, and uncertainties, and writing a book in this moment wasn't easy, and I would never have been able to do it without the priceless support of my family and friends to whom all my love and gratitude goes. Thank you for being always close even when you were far.

A special thanks to my sister Daniela who cycled many kilometers just to check on me and have wonderful social distanced chats in the park and also managed to organize the best virtual birthday during lockdown with all the big family from Italy, including my dear grandma Maria. Thank you so much! You are my rock.

Warmest thanks to Elena, Andrea, Nora and Federica for always being there and gifting me with their precious friendship.

I want to take the opportunity to thank the Red Cross volunteers, healthcare workers, and everyone who worked hard to help us all during the COVID-19 pandemic. Thank you all!

Thanks to the amazing Apress team and to the great people at Feral Interactive for their support, friendship and humanity in such a challenging moment.

Finally, thanks to you who bought this book and are about to start your journey into game AI. I hope that this little book will help you reach your goals.

Introduction

In this book, you will learn what Artificial Intelligence is and how to build an intelligent agent.

We will cover the fundamentals of game AI programming starting from creating the fundamentals of linear algebra, moving to pathfinding and search algorithms to create agents that can navigate into complex 3D worlds, and finally landing in the world of behavior programming to build fun and interesting NPCs.

Let's take a closer look to what each chapter is going to cover.

Chapter 1, Introduction

This chapter is an introduction to the topics we are about to explore, with some important definition and background information about AI and more importantly AI in video games.

Chapter 2, The Basics

In this chapter, we will explore the fundamentals of 3D math with a brief introduction to some important concepts of linear algebra.

This chapter is essential to understand how you can make objects move in a 3D space.

In this chapter, we will build a simple NPC that will move toward a point in a 3D plane with no obstacles by just applying linear algebra.

Chapter 3, Paths and Waypoints

In this chapter, we will talk about pathfinding, one of the foundations of AI. We will start with a quick introduction to graph theory, and we will introduce some important algorithms and how to use them to solve game-related problems.

In this chapter, we will introduce the navigation problem by building an NPC capable of navigating in a maze using a waypoint system and pathfinding algorithms.

Chapter 4, Navigation

In this chapter, we will continue the talk about navigation. We will introduce the de facto standard to solve navigation problems: applying A* to a NavMesh.

In this chapter, we will create an NPC capable of reaching any walkable part of a 3D map (with obstacles) by finding the shortest path from its starting point to the user's selected goal.

Chapter 5, Behaviors

In this chapter, you will learn how to tackle the challenge of creating an intelligent (or apparently so) NPC able to behave differently according to the environment and the situation in which it is in by using Finite-State Machines.

In this chapter, we will build a mini stealth game featuring a labyrinth and a guard that will patrol the area looking for the player and chasing them. You will learn how to implement a cone view to make the agent perceive the environment and how to implement various behaviors and to trigger them according to the situation.

CHAPTER 1

Introduction

Among all the technologies that have been flourishing in the last decade, there is one that is becoming essential for our society and it's enhancing all the other tech fields as well as every aspect of our life: Artificial Intelligence (AI). From navigation systems to smart cars and from virtual assistants to augmented reality (AR) applications on our smartphones, nearly every software and device we use features AI under the hood. Video games make no exception.

The more we go on, the more AI is present in game applications in the form of non-player character (NPC), simulations, and more recently AR applications aiming to enhance the user experience. Machine learning algorithms are starting to be a common solution to enhance graphics and animations or even implement new gameplay features.

In this chapter, I will briefly present to you Artificial Intelligence and talk about its relationship with video games. Finally, I will present to you what this book has to offer for you and what to expect from it.

Let's start with the basic question: What is Artificial Intelligence?

1.1 Artificial Intelligence

Intelligence is the trait that we, as humans, are most interested in. We survived in the feral world thanks to our intelligence that allowed us to impose ourselves on animals and the environment itself by understanding the laws of nature and how to craft and use tools to take advantage of them to sustain our species.

© Sebastiano M. Cossu 2021
S. M. Cossu, *Beginning Game AI with Unity*,
https://doi.org/10.1007/978-1-4842-6355-6_1

Thanks to our intelligence, we managed not only to survive but to evolve and build a world that would maximize our chances of survival, creating complex organizational systems to satisfy all our needs.

This is why we value intelligence so much even now. We judge people by their intelligence; we value them by their ability to think out of the box and optimize processes or get the best results in some specific process. To us, intelligence is not only the ability to think, but more importantly it's the ability to perceive and understand the world that surrounds us and act in order to exploit it to reach our goals.

Intelligence is the blessing that Nature gifted us, and with Artificial Intelligence, we aim to pass the torch to our own creations: machines.

It's still debated if Artificial Intelligence is more about making machines think and act like humans or if it's about creating machines with the gift of rational thinking that do things purposefully in the best possible way exploiting the environment. Both the directions are completely legit, and they are leading to very interesting results. In this book, we will explore the interpretation of AI intended to create rational agents that can process the perceptions from the environment and elaborate them applying a reasoning process to come up with a solution (an action or a sequence of them) to solve a complex problem.

In the next section, we will see more in detail what is an intelligent agent and in which applications they are involved.

1.1.1 Intelligent Agents

An intelligent agent is the combination of an intelligent system and an agent.

An intelligent system is an apparatus capable of processing information in order to reach a specific goal, while an agent is something that acts and reacts to the information it receives. Therefore, an intelligent agent is a system capable of processing perceived information and taking action in order to reach a specific goal.

An agent is made of *sensors* to perceive the environment and *actuators* that allow them to take action (Figure 1-1).

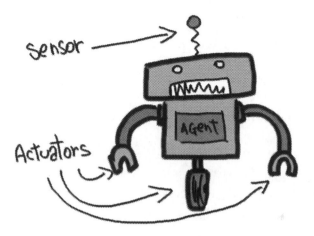

Figure 1-1. *An agent has sensors to perceive the environment and actuators to act on it*

It's easy to picture in our head an intelligent agent as a robot with devices like photocells, cameras, antennas, or other kinds of sensors to perceive the environment, a computer to elaborate information and to come out with an action that will be executed using some kind of actuators, like robotic arms, wheels, or other kinds of mechanisms to interact with the world.

From a mathematical point of view, an intelligent agent can be seen as a function where the arguments are perceptions; the logic of the function allows the elaboration of perceptions which takes to a result (the return value) which is the final action to be taken.

This can be represented by the following definition:

$$\to\to\ P^* \to A$$

which means that an agent function $\to$ maps every possible percept sequence P* to an appropriate action A. Obviously, this concept is easily representable in a programming language, and it will be the foundation of our work to create intelligent agents with Unity.

Before starting to talk about Unity, the game engine we will use to explore AI, let's see how AI and intelligent agents relate to the world of video games.

1.1.2 AI in Video Games

From the very beginning of the history of video games, AI was part of it. In fact, one of the very first AI applications were intelligent agents capable of playing games by their own both against other AIs and humans. That kind of intelligent agents are just programs that can play a game by themselves without the help of humans. Their goal is to make the best choices to win the game. They perceive the game environment, elaborate the collected data, and come out with the most convenient action.

Autonomous playing agents had their first great victory in 1997 when Deep Blue, the AI built by IBM, defeated the world champion Garry Kasparov in a game of chess. Kasparov commented on that game saying, "That day I sensed a new kind of intelligence."

Today, winning a game of chess against an AI is just impossible. Another more recent victory of the AI against humans was registered in 2011 when Watson, the new AI built by IBM, won by a long shot at *Jeopardy!* against human players. Watson's achievement was way more impressive than Deep Blue's because to win *Jeopardy!*, you need to have a great knowledge of pop culture and be able to link facts in fields like music, gossip, cinema, and so on. While we expect an Artificial Intelligence to be good at rational reasoning activities like math and chess, we don't expect them to have a better understanding of our culture, which Watson proved to have – this is what made that achievement so important.

With the increasing popularity of video games, in the 1970s, AI started to focus on creating compelling enemies for single-player games. Some of the first games to do so were *Speed Race* (Taito, 1974), *Qwak!* (Atari, 1974), and *Pursuit* (Kee Games, 1975). Following those precursors, in the so-called Golden Age of video games, AI started to become more popular and common in video games, and some of the first interesting applications started to show up, for example, the acrobatic maneuvers of enemies breaking out of formations in games like *Galaxian* (Namco, 1979) and *Galaga* (Namco, 1981) or the original approach of *Pac-Man* (Namco, 1980) in which the enemies had distinct personalities and tried to chase the player by combining efforts and using actual strategies based on pathfinding techniques and application of patterns to chase the player.

Following the popularity of AI applications in the Golden Age, video games started to implement intelligent behaviors featuring increased complexity. In particular, those were the years in which tactical and action RPG started to show up with games like *Dragon Quest IV*, *Baldur's Gate*, and *Secret of Mana* which implemented some interesting new features, like the possibility to issue orders and set behaviors for the members of the party so that they could fight in battles in autonomy. Other interesting techniques started to rise to simulate team efforts in sports games too. Raising the complexity of the applications, the limits of the current technologies started to show up, and more complex solutions were found. In particular, the 1990s were the years in which video games started to implement formal AI techniques. Finite-State Machine (FSM) is one of those, and it was (and still is) one of the most popular. FSM can elegantly solve a broad set of problems affecting nearly every game genre, but probably the most popular applications are enemies' behaviours in action games; in this type of games, enemies have to react to situations and execute appropriate actions, and those behaviors can be represented as FSMs.

The most popular examples of video games using FSM are *Pac-Man* (Namco, 1980) and *Ms. Pac-Man* (Namco, 1981). They introduced the concept of enemies adapting to different situations and changing their behaviors deciding to chase or flee the player. But that's not all; in fact, *Pac-Man* and Ms Pac-Man were also the first games where the enemies were looking like they were collaborating towards the common goal of defeating the player.

In fact, the enemies in both games were four different ghosts with four different personalities, and they were following complementary strategies to chase the player, making them looking like they were actually collaborating following a big and well organized chasing plan. All this was achieved thanks to FSM which is basically a graph where you associate states to actions, making the NPC take a specific action according to the state it (or the game world) is in. This way, the player has the impression that the NPC is actually thinking and reacting rationally to a specific situation.

The Finite State Machine is not a thing of the past, in fact, we can still find it in very modern and complex games like the Tomb Raider series of games or the Battlefield or Call of Duty series of games. Generally, most of the action games are implementing FSM to manage their NPCs' behaviours. This is because FSM is easy to implement and has low impact on performances, and yet it provides a genuine and credible user experience when well designed. Other AI approaches require many more resources and work, and in some game genres and situations, they don't even create a more immersive or credible result compared to their FSM equivalent.

In today's video games, AI is not only used to create intelligent agents. We are recently seeing the rise of augmented reality (AR) which uses computer vision techniques to enhance objects in the real world with virtual elements. One of the most important applications of that kind is *Pokémon Go* (Niantic, 2016), which allows players to see and catch Pokémons in the real world using a smartphone.

Other interesting applications of AI in video games arise with the advancement and popularity of machine learning, which is used to enhance graphics and gameplay elements in many new video games. A very interesting example can be seen in Warframe (Digital Extremes, 2013), where a machine learning algorithm is used to teach the enemies how to wall-run by observing the players doing it and processing that data to mark all the runnable walls and the starting and landing points for those wall-runs.

There were some famous examples of more advanced AI techniques used in video games, like the Creatures series of games by Steve Grand that created one of the most famous and important Artificial Life (AL) games, which is still today remembered as one of the most complex and genius AL games. Creatures used many interesting AI techniques like genetics algorithms and neural networks to create virtual-biological beings that could transmit their genetic traits to their offspring by mating and that were able to learn by experimenting in their environment and learning from the consequences of their actions. This is one of the most interesting and important products of AL, and I strongly suggest you to buy and play the game and to read the book written by Steve Grand about the making of the game: *Creation: Life and How to Make It.*

No doubt, AI is becoming more and more important to enhance the overall experience of video games in many different ways and to keep up with all the changes and evolutions brought by AI. It's wise to start learning from the very beginning; this means understanding how to create basic intelligent agents. To reach this goal, we will make use of many different tools belonging to Computer Science and Math. The concepts explained will be implemented in Unity using the C# programming language. For simplicity's sake, we will not use complex 3D models, but only very basic 3D objects (mostly geometrical 3D shapes like cubes and spheres) as the focus here is not to make a nice-looking video game, but to understand useful game AI techniques to reuse and adapt to any game project.

1.2 Unity

Unity needs no introductions. It's probably the most popular game engine around, and it helped making game development more accessible to indie developers and small studios.

Our choice to use Unity is mostly dictated by its simplicity and completeness. It's a game engine that's very easy to pick up, but at the same time, it features many advanced tools, and its libraries offer many interesting and useful functions that will make our work way easier, letting us concentrate on the interesting parts.

In Unity, you program using C#, an OOP language that offers many advanced features packed in a gorgeous C-like syntax. It is an extremely powerful and clear programming language that allows us to achieve complex goals with smart tools and clarity. Moreover, it's the best choice if we want to use all the features that Unity has to offer. Last but not least, it's based on the object-oriented programming (OOP) paradigm, which allows for more structured and modular coding style.

All those characteristics make C# a good choice for this book not only because it's a good tool to get the work done but also because it's extremely good to learn coding and master some techniques we are going to use in the book.

The first step to get the benefits of using Unity and C# is to actually install Unity, so let's see how to do it!

1.2.1 Installing Unity Hub

Unity is a free software; the first step to get it installed on your machine is to download Unity Hub from the official website: `https://stsssore.unity.com/download`.

Unity Hub is the software that will help you organize and keep track of all your Unity projects and Unity versions. With Unity Hub, you can install or uninstall specific versions of Unity and add or remove Unity projects and link them to specific versions of Unity very easily.

Once on the download page, you will be asked to accept the license agreement, after which it will be possible to click the download button to get the installer.

After downloading the installer, you will need to follow a different process depending on whether you are installing it on Windows, Mac, or Linux:

- On Windows, you have to accept the license agreement and choose a path on your drive on which you want Unity Hub to be installed, then press "Install" and the software will get your machine the latest version of the Unity Hub software.

- On Mac, you just need to drag the app into your Application folder, as usual.

- On Linux, you will need to open the Unity Hub installer (which in this case is an AppImage file) with the AppImage file Launcher.

1.2.2 Activating Your Unity ID and License

Starting Unity Hub for the first time, you will be prompted to the License Management window: here, you will be asked to activate a license to start using Unity (Figure 1-2).

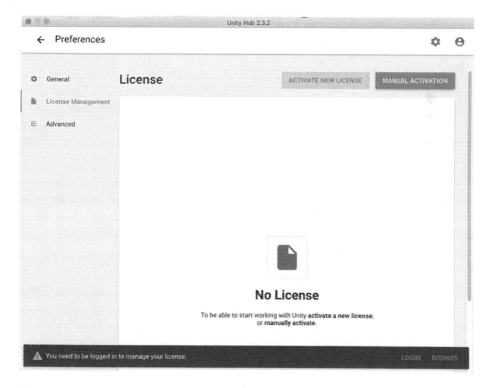

Figure 1-2. *License Management window. You need to have a Unity ID and activate a license to start using Unity*

Before you do that, you need to create a free Unity account, which you can do by clicking the Unity ID icon on the top right of the screen and selecting Sign In (Figure 1-3) and "create one" (Figure 1-4).

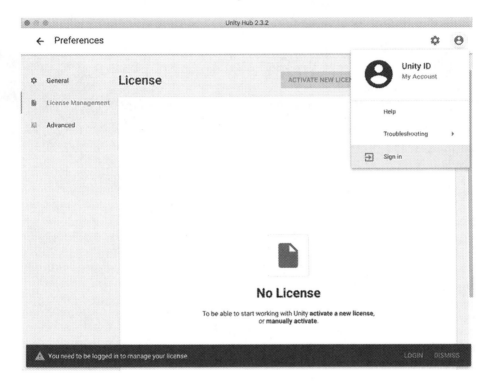

Figure 1-3. *Click the Unity ID icon and then Sign In to log in or register your Unity ID*

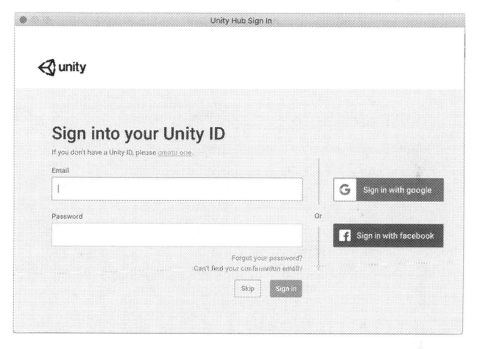

Figure 1-4. *This is the log-in form; click "create one" to register a Unity ID*

A new window containing a registration form will open up (Figure 1-5). Just fill the form or use one of the two buttons if you rather register using your Google or Facebook account.

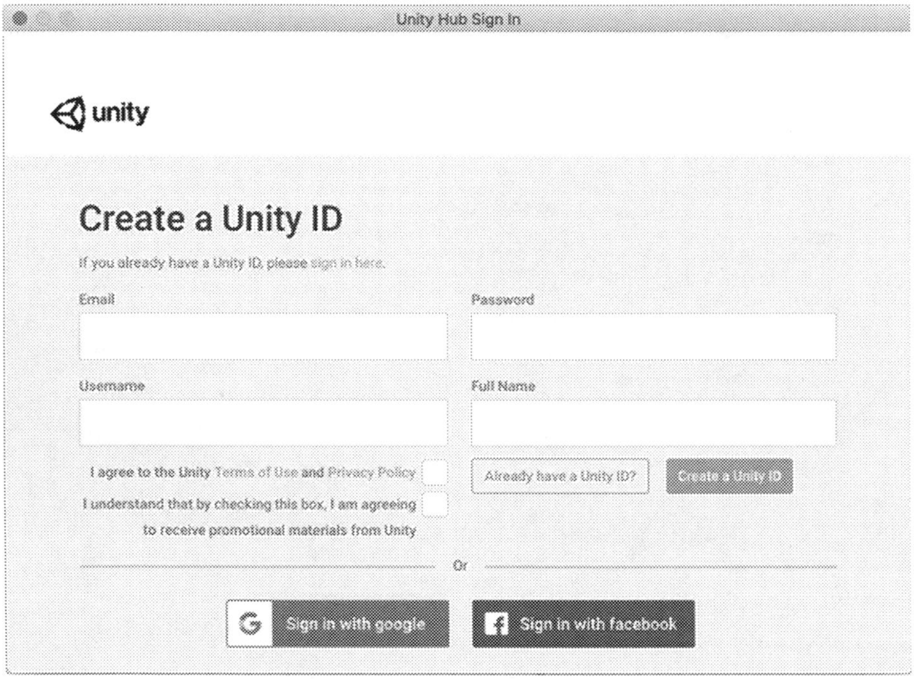

Figure 1-5. *Fill this form to create a Unity ID, or click the buttons at the bottom of the window if you want to create it using your Google or Facebook account*

Now that you are logged in with your Unity ID, you can activate a license. You can do that in the License Management window (Figure 1-6) in two ways:

- **Manual Activation**: This is useful if you don't have an active connection to the Internet. You can create a license request file and upload it later to `https://license.unity3d.com/manual`.

- **Guided Activation**: You need to follow some steps and answer some questions to automatically activate a license on your Unity ID.

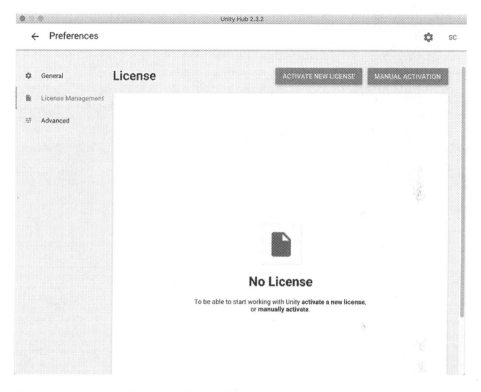

Figure 1-6. *Now that you logged in your Unity ID, you can request a license with one of the two blue buttons in the top right of the window*

1.2.2.1 Manual Activation

If you want to activate your license manually, click the Manual Activation button in the License Management section (Figure 1-6). You will be prompted with a small window asking you to generate and save a license request file to be later uploaded on https://license.unity3d.com/manual (Figure 1-7). Click the "SAVE LICENSE REQUEST" button and save the license request file on your computer (Figure 1-8).

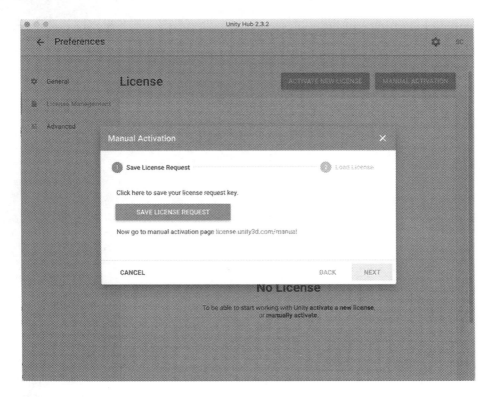

Figure 1-7. *Manual Activation view. Here, you can request your license to be later uploaded on* https://license.unity3d.com/manual

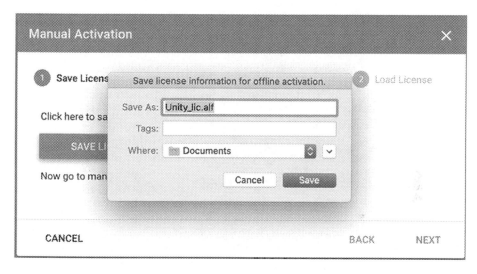

Figure 1-8. *Save your license request file and upload it on* `https://` `license.unity3d.com/manual`

After saving the file on your computer, you need to go to `https://` `license.unity3d.com/manual` and upload the file you just saved (Figure 1-9) to the uploading form and then press the Next button.

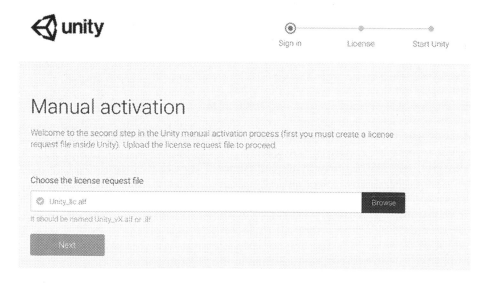

Figure 1-9. *Uploading the license request file on* `https://license.` `unity3d.com/manual`

Uploading your license request will activate your account automatically for your Unity ID in Unity Hub, allowing you to download Unity on your PC and start using it.

1.2.2.2 Guided Activation

The guided activation needs you to have a working Internet connection, but it's faster and easier.

You need to click "Activate New License" in the window shown in Figure 1-6; then you will be presented with a new window asking you what kind of license you want to activate (Figure 1-10) and if you plan to use Unity for commercial or learning purposes (Figure 1-11). Make your choice based on your use case and then click "Done."

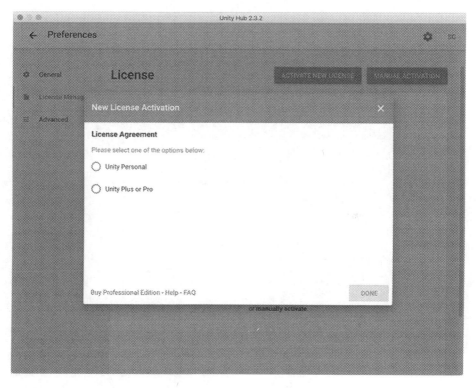

Figure 1-10. *You can choose between two classes of licenses: Unity Personal (made for individuals and amateurs) and Unity Plus or Pro (made for professionals)*

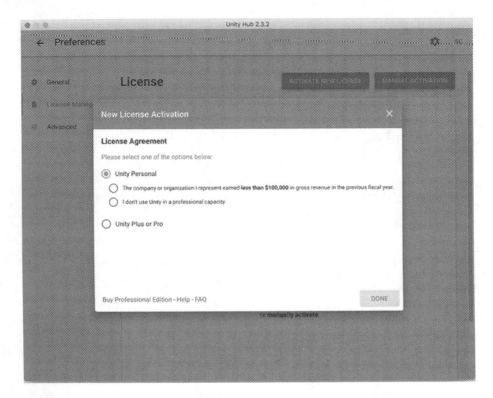

Figure 1-11. *You can use Unity for free, if you don't plan to sell your game, but there are also interesting plans if your company earns less than a certain amount*

After completing all the steps, the License Management window will contain the details of your new active license, meaning you are all set up (Figure 1-12).

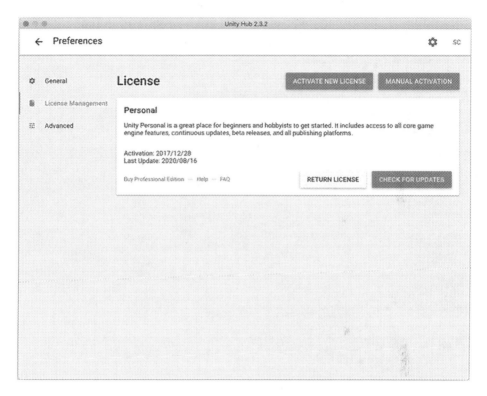

Figure 1-12. *A new license was activated, and Unity Hub is now ready to be used!*

1.2.2.3 Installing Unity

After activating your Unity ID and license, you need to download a version of Unity from Unity Hub.

Click Installs in the left side of the window, and you will be prompted to the Installs *view* which should list all the available versions of Unity installed on the computer (Figure 1-13).

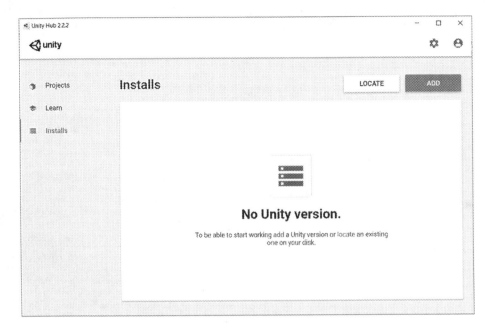

Figure 1-13. *This is the Installs view. Here, you can add or delete different versions of Unity*

From the Installs view, click the Add button to select a new version of Unity to install and a pop-up listing all the available versions of Unity will be shown as in Figure 1-14.

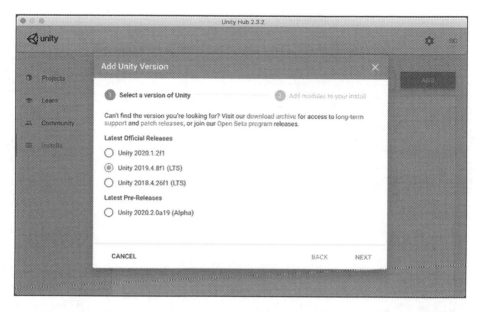

Figure 1-14. *The first step to install Unity asks you to pick a version of the engine*

To follow this book, you will not be forced to use a specific version of Unity, since we are not going to use any specific feature of the software; anyway, the UI of the engine may differ from version to version, so I suggest you to not use a version older than the LTS version of 2018. I will be using the LTS version from 2019 for this book.

Once you select the right version of Unity, click the Next button.

Once you selected the right version and clicked Next, you will be asked to choose which modules to install (Figure 1-15). Those modules will allow you to export your project to several different platforms, from desktop to mobile and the Web and others a bit more specific like tvOS and Vuforia.

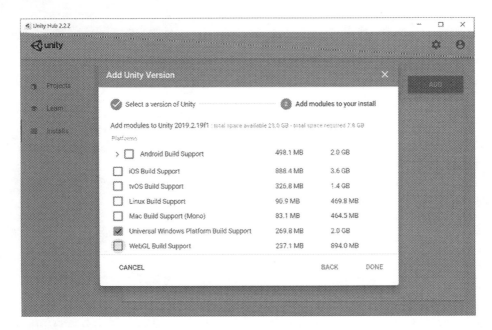

Figure 1-15. *The second step to install Unity asks you to choose which modules you want to install. Those modules will allow you to export your project to many different platforms*

For this book, we will only export on desktop, so select the module related to the desktop operating system (OS) you are using. For example, if you are using a Mac, you may want to install the Mac Build Support module; if you're using Linux, install Linux Build Support; and if you're on Windows (as myself), install Windows Build Support. I also suggest you to install the Documentation module which is always useful to have locally on your PC.

Finally, click the Done button to conclude the process and start downloading and installing the version of Unity you just selected.

CHAPTER 2

The Basics

As cleverly explained in the book *Flatland* by Edwin Abbott, reality is made by many dimensions, and depending on your perception skills, you can see and act only on some of them. This is true also in video games: video games can be set in 3D or 2D worlds, and this distinction determines the way in which agents can perceive the surrounding world and so their ability to move and act.

An N-dimensional space is a geometrical setting in which a point in space is identified by N values or parameters, commonly named after the last letters of the alphabet.

In a two-dimensional space (2D space or plane), a point in space is defined by two values called width and height (commonly referred to as x and y). The objects you can represent in a 2D space are points, lines, and all the plane geometrical figures like triangles, squares, circles, and so on (Figure 2-1).

© Sebastiano M. Cossu 2021
S. M. Cossu, *Beginning Game AI with Unity*,
https://doi.org/10.1007/978-1-4842-6355-6_2

Figure 2-1. *A 2D space has two dimensions: width and height*

In a three-dimensional space (3D space) – which is the space we can perceive – points in space are identified by three parameters: height, width, and depth, commonly referred to as x, y, z. In a 3D space, you can represent all the 2D objects and all the objects that, other than height and width, have also the third dimension: depth. Geometrical objects that have three dimensions are cubes, spheres, pyramids, and…well, basically all the matter we know in the universe (Figure 2-2)!

Figure 2-2. *A 3D space has three dimensions: width, height, and depth*

So, as we said, depending on the number of dimensions in a space, you need an adequate number of values to identify a point in that space. Those values are represented by vectors.

2.1 Vectors

A vector is a quantity defined in an N-space by n values, and it has magnitude and direction. The magnitude of a vector is basically the size of the vector, while the direction is its orientation in the space (Figure 2-3).

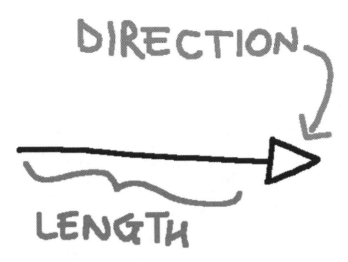

Figure 2-3. *A basic representation of a vector*

A straightforward example of a vector is acceleration. Let's say you're driving a car at 50 km/h. If you keep going at 50 km/h, the acceleration is 0 km/h^2; if you press the accelerator a bit more, the velocity will grow at a pace of – let's say – 5 km/h^2. This acceleration value is a vector with direction equal to the orientation of the car and magnitude 5 km/h^2.

So, with vectors, we can track movements and forces acting in a space. For example, in a video game (2D or 3D, doesn't matter), the movement of a character moving from a point A to a point B is represented by a vector $\overrightarrow{AB}$ of magnitude m = B-A and direction equal to the orientation of an arrow going from A to B (Figure 2-4).

Figure 2-4. *The arrow represents the movement vector of a character in a 2D platformer*

In Unity, vectors are represented using specific data types. You can define a 2D vector by using Vector2 and a 3D vector by using Vector3.

You can declare them using their constructor as follows:

```
Vector2 my2DVector = new Vector2(x, y);
Vector3 my3DVector = new Vector3(x, y, z);
```

Vectors are at the core of every operation in an N-space, both in linear algebra and in Unity. For example, the position of an object is represented by a 3D vector as well as its scale value. Those two values can be modified via vector operations. Let's take a quick look at the most important operations with vectors and their meaning in the video game context.

2.1.1 Addition

The addition between two vectors of the same type (e.g., two 3D vectors) is made by calculating the sum of the components of the two vectors as shown in Figure 2-5.

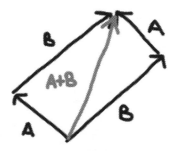

Figure 2-5. *A graphical representation of the sum between two vectors A and B*

So if, for example, you want to sum the two vectors [1, 2, 3] and [4, 5, 6], you just calculate the resulting vector [1+4, 2+5, 3+6] which is [5, 7, 9].

Since a vector can represent a point in space, the sum between two vectors is used to represent a movement from that point to a new point in the space. So, basically, when you sum a vector A to a vector B, the vector A is going to be the starting point, and the vector B is the offset that leads you to the new point C = A+B.

In Unity, you can sum two vectors by using the + (plus) operator like this:

```
Vector3 result = new Vector3(1,2,3) + new Vector3(4,5,6);
```

2.1.2 Subtraction

Subtraction between two vectors is pretty similar to addition. The only different thing is that the direction of the second element is reversed.

For example, if you want to calculate the difference between a vector A = [4,5,6] and a vector B = [1,2,3], you have to calculate the resulting vector C = A - B = [4,5,6] - [1,2,3] = [4,5,6] + [-1,-2,-3] = [4-1, 5-2, 6-3] = [3, 3, 3].

The subtraction between two vectors is used to find out the difference between them, which, in a spatial context, represents the distance between the two points represented by the two vectors.

In Unity, you can subtract two vectors by using the - (minus) operator like this:

```
Vector3 result = new Vector3(4,5,6) - new Vector(1,2,3);
```

2.1.3 Scalar Multiplication

As we said, a vector has a magnitude and a direction. The magnitude is the length of the vector.

To calculate the magnitude |V| of a vector V = [a, b, c], we apply the following formula:

$$|V| = \sqrt{a^2 + b^2 + c^2}$$

You can change the magnitude of a vector by just multiplying or dividing all the values of the vector by the desired quantity. Figure 2-6 shows a graphical representation of the scalar multiplication on a vector.

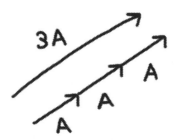

Figure 2-6. *A graphical representation of a scalar multiplication on a vector*

For example, if you want to double the magnitude of the vector V = [1, 2, 3] by a scalar value x = 2, you can just multiply each of V's elements by x, like this: V*x = [1*2, 2*2, 3*2] = [2, 4, 6].

Similarly, if you want to reduce the magnitude of a vector W = [2, 4, 6] by a scalar value x = 2, you can just divide each of W's elements by x, like this: W/x = [2/2, 4/2, 6/2] = [1, 2, 3].

2.1.4 Dot Product

Another important operation on vectors is the dot product. This is an algebraic operation you can execute on two vectors to get a scalar value. The result of a dot product between two vectors is the difference between the directions they're facing.

Generally, the dot product is applied to normalized vectors, which are vectors of length 1. This is because when we want to calculate the difference between the directions of two vectors, we don't care much about their length, but only about their direction.

When you apply the dot product to a couple of normalized vectors, the result is included in the range between 1 and -1. If the resulting value is 1, the two vectors face the same direction; if it's 0, they are perpendicular; if it's -1, they face opposite directions (Figure 2-7).

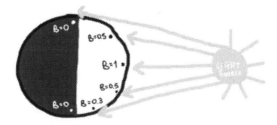

Figure 2-7. *Dot product is very useful to calculate values like the brightness in a 3D space*

One of the practical applications the dot product can have is to calculate the brightness on a surface based on the position of the light source. Let L be the light vector, which represents the position and direction of the light source, and N the vector representing the normal vector to a surface (meaning the vector perpendicular to a surface). Calculating B = L dot N will give us B as a float number representing the brightness of the surface of which N is the normal vector, where a value less or equal to 0 means darkness and a 1 means maximum brightness.

In Unity, you can calculate the dot product of the two vectors L and N we talked about in the previous example, using Vector3's dot function like this:

```
float B = Vector3.Dot(N, L);
```

2.2 The First Project!

Previously, we said how vectors are used to represent positions and directions. Let's put this in practice using Unity!

Open up Unity and create a new project by clicking the New button (Figure 2-8).

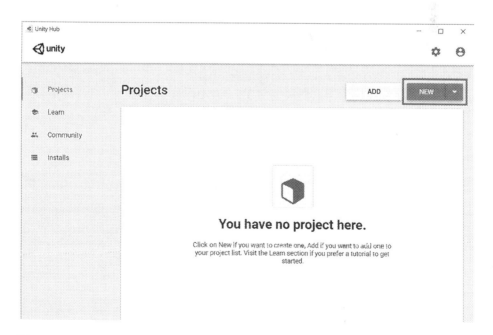

Figure 2-8. *Create a new project in Unity Hub*

From the template list, select the 3D project template and choose a name and a folder for your new project as shown in Figure 2-9, then click Create.

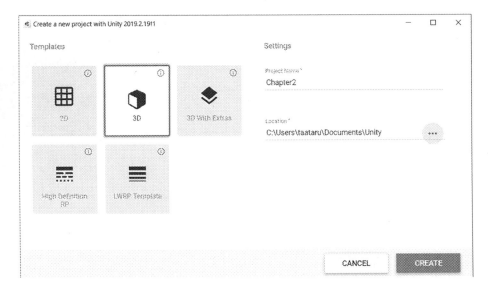

Figure 2-9. *Create a 3D project in Unity Hub*

Unity will set up a project for you in seconds.

When the project is created, you will be shown the classic layout with different sections dedicated to different parts of the project. Let's explore the main ones! The following list refers to Figures 2-10 and 2-11:

1. **Toolbar**: It gives you access to some essential features like tools to manipulate the Scene View and the Game Objects in it, the buttons to run and stop the game as well as the step button to debug it, the buttons to access cloud services and versioning features.

2. **Hierarchy Window**: It shows the list of all the objects in the current scene. From the hierarchy panel, you can access every single object and modify their properties via the Inspector.

3. **Inspector Window**: The Inspector shows you all the details related to the asset currently selected. This window has not a standard view, as different kinds of assets have different kinds of properties.

4. **Project Window**: It's basically an assets explorer showing and listing all the assets related to your projects. As new assets will be created, they will be shown in the Project window.

5. **Scene View**: It shows the selected scene and allows you to navigate it and edit the Game Objects within it. You can interact with the scene in the Scene View in 3D or 2D mode by selecting the corresponding button.

6. **Game View**: It allows you to see what your final rendered game will look like. Pressing the Play button, you can start the game in this view.

7. **Console Window**: It shows errors, warnings, and other messages generated by Unity or custom messages created by the programmer using the Debug.Log, Debug.LogWarning, and Debug. LogError functions.

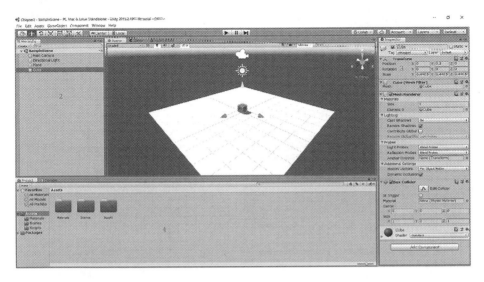

Figure 2-10. *The figure shows some important parts of the Unity Editor UI (find the explanations in the preceding numbered list)*

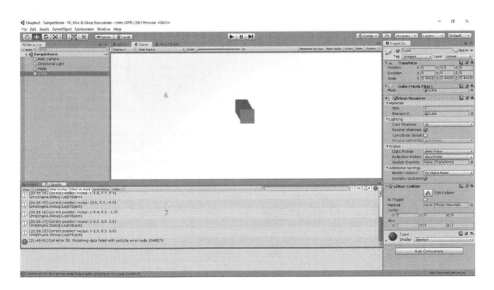

Figure 2-11. *The figure shows some important parts of the Unity Editor UI (find the explanations in the preceding numbered list)*

2.2.1 The First Scene!

In our first project, we want to explore the basics of vectors by creating an application that allows us to move an object around by modifying its position vector. The application will consist of a plane with a simple cube on it. Using the mouse, we can click different parts of the plane and change the position of the cube modifying its position vector.

As you may imagine, 3D objects are defined in a 3D space by the 3D position vectors of their vertices. In Unity, though, for simplicity, we will only need to modify a single vector called the pivot point. The pivot point is a vector associated with an object representing its position in the 3D space.

So, let's get started by adding a couple of 3D objects to our starting Scene.

Right-click the hierarchy or the assets panel and select 3D Object ➤ Plane from the contextual menu. This will create a plane in the Scene.

Now, we want to change the position of our plane, so that we can have it exactly in the center of the scene. To do that, we need to modify the pivot point, which – as we just said – is a 3D vector. Left-click the plane in the Hierarchy window, and the info and properties of the object will be shown in the Inspector panel. Locate the **Transform** section and change the x, y, z properties to x = 0, y = 0, z = 0. This will snap our plane in the origin of the scene (Figure 2-12).

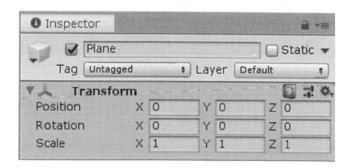

Figure 2-12. *The plane object as seen in the Inspector*

> **Tip**   The origin is the point 0 of any N-space. In the case of a 2D space, like a Cartesian plane, the origin is at position x = 0, y = 0. In a 3D space, like our Scene in Unity, it's at position x = 0, y = 0, z = 0.

Now create a cube in the same way, by right-clicking the assets or hierarchy panel and selecting 3D object ➤ cube. Select the cube by left-clicking it in the Hierarchy window to make its property be listed in the Inspector page. There, change the values of x, y, and z properties of the Transform position section to x = 0, y = 0.3, and z = 0 (Figure 2-13).

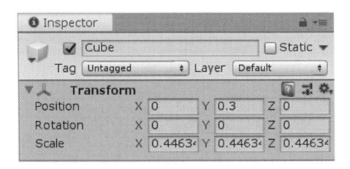

Figure 2-13.   *The Cube object as seen in the Inspector*

Now that we have our 3D objects in place, the only thing we need is a good point of view! The visible scene, in a game, is defined by the Camera object, which is a GameObject that consists of many properties that allow you to show your game world from different points of view and with different graphic settings. Anyway, we won't get too deep in this because it would take us too far from the scope of this book. The only thing we need to know is that a Camera allows us to define what we can see and how. Once again, the position of the camera is defined by a vector that we need to modify.

Select the Main Camera object in the Hierarchy window, navigate to the Transform Position section of the Inspector, and change its x, y, z properties to x = 0, y = 4, z = 0. In the Inspector, locate the Transform Rotation property and set x, y, and z to x = 90, y = 0, and z = 0 (Figure 2-14).

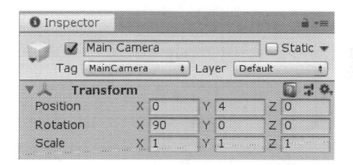

Figure 2-14. *The Main Camera as seen in the Inspector*

OK, now the scene is complete! We have the camera looking down at the plane with the cube in its center. We need now to add the functionality to make the cube move to the different positions at which we will point with the mouse. We can do this using C# scripting. Let's see how!

2.2.2 The First Script!

As you know if you already worked with Unity, scripting is made by writing script files and assigning them to objects. Every script can implement standard functions that define the moment in which the actions are executed. What we want to do is to constantly check the position of the mouse, and if the user clicks, we want the cube to move to those coordinates.

Create the script by right-clicking the Project window and selecting Create ► C# Script. Rename the script to Move. Now double-click the script to open the text editor and start writing the code.

The script you just created would contain this template code:

```
1.    using System.Collections;
2.    using System.Collections.Generic;
3.    using UnityEngine;
4
5     public class Move : MonoBehaviour
6     {
7         // Start is called before the first frame update
8         void Start()
9         {
10
11        }
12
13        // Update is called once per frame
14        void Update()
15        {
16
17        }
18    }
```

Lines 1–3 are just lines to include some libraries and modules. The interesting part starts just after: a new class with the name of the file is declared inheriting from the class MonoBehaviour (**line 5**); this allows us to override some useful methods like Start (**line 8**) that is called every time the game starts and Update (**line 14**) that is called every frame. We can get rid of the Start function, as we won't use it.

The plan is to wait for the user to click a point in the space and then read the coordinate of the mouse cursor and move the cube to those coordinates. To do that, we will make use of the raycasting technique, which is widely used in Unity for so many purposes. Every frame, we will cast a ray from the camera to the mouse position, and when the user clicks, we will calculate the position at which the ray collides with the 3D plane and move the cube to that position.

The first thing to do is to assign the script we just created to the cube object, so find that object in the Hierarchy window and select it by clicking it. The properties for that object will be shown in the Inspector. Now drag the Move script and drop it in the Hierarchy window showing the cube's properties. That's it! Now your script is associated to that object (Figure 2-15).

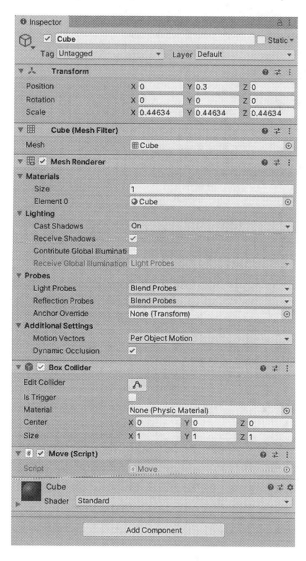

Figure 2-15. *The Cube object as seen in the Inspector with all its settings listed*

Now that the script is associated with the cube, we can start modifying it and adding the functionality. Double-click the script to open it up in your favorite editor/IDE and replace the content with the following code:

```
1.    using UnityEngine;
2.
3.    public class Move : MonoBehaviour
4.    {
5.        private void Update()
6.        {
7.            RaycastHit hit;
8.            Ray ray = Camera.main.ScreenPointToRay(Input.
                mousePosition);
9.            if (Physics.Raycast(ray, out hit) && Input.
                GetMouseButtonDown(0))
10.            {
11.                Vector3 newPosition = new Vector3(hit.
                    point.x, this.transform.position.y, hit.
                    point.z);
12.                this.transform.position = newPosition;
13.                Debug.Log("Current position vector: " +
                    newPosition.ToString());
14.            }
15.        }
16.    }
```

This is the full code to add the functionality we talked about; let's analyze it better!

We already saw the structure of the file, with the using statement and the class declaration. We won't need the Start method, so we can just get rid of it. We will only need the Update method; let's see how!

At **line 7**, we declare the `hit` variable of type `RaycastHit`. This is a structure used to get information from a `ray` collision against a `Collider`.

The idea is to cast a ray from the camera to the coordinates of the cursor in the moment the user clicks. The collision point between the ray and the first collider – in this case, the collider of the 3D plane – will be stored inside the `hit` variable. This will allow us to calculate the position we want the cube to move to.

At **line 8**, we create the `ray` variable of type `Ray`: this is the actual ray we are going to shoot from the camera to the mouse position via the function `ScreenPointToRay` passing as argument the position of the mouse contained in the vector `Input.mousePosition`.

At **line 9**, we call the `Physics.Raycast(ray, out hit)` function that casts the ray from the camera to the mouse position. That function returns `true` if the ray hit a collider, and the hit position is stored in the `hit` variable we passed to the function. In the same line, we also call the `Input.GetMouseButtonDown(0)` function that returns `true` if the mouse button indexed with 0 is pressed. As you can imagine, by default, the mouse indexed as 0 is the primary button: the left button; the right button is indexed as 1 and the middle button as 2. We put those two function calls in conjunction using the AND operator.; if both return true, we execute the instructions from **lines 11 to 13**.

At **line 11**, we create the new position vector using the x and z coordinates we found in the *hit* variable (the coordinates at which the ray hit the collider of the 3D plane) and for the y coordinate, we use the one of the cube object so we can keep it at the same height.

At **line 12**, we assign the position vector to the current object's position, and at **line 13** we print that information to the debug console using the `Debug.Log` function, just to see the position vector values changing.

Now that we have our very first script, we can now play the game and test it. Press the play button to compile and run the game. You will be presented with the scene and the cube at the center (Figure 2-16). Click any place in the 3D plane to move the cube there.

Figure 2-16. *Playing the game, you will start with the cube at the center. When you click a spot, the cube will move there*

Now that we explored the vectors a bit also in practice, let's take a step further. It would be nice to make the cube move toward the point we click, instead of just teleporting it there. Let's see how we can do this.

2.2.3 Moving Toward a Point

In the previous section, we managed to move the cube instantly to a certain position that we selected with the click of the mouse. What we want to achieve in this section is to move it gradually toward the point selected in a certain amount of time. The basic difference is that instead of moving to that point all in one movement, the object will make several small steps toward the goal position.

We want to recreate the idea of movement in space from a point A to a point B in a certain span of time; to do that, we can use the concept of **geometric translation**.

Geometric translation is a geometric transformation that moves all the points of a figure or a space in the same direction. The movement is achieved by adding a constant vector to every point of the figure; that constant vector is the movement vector, which defines the point in space we want to reach.

In Unity, we have the Translate method of the Transform class that implements exactly the concept of geometrical translation. Every object in a scene in Unity has a Transform, which allows for storing and manipulating the position, rotation, and scale of the object.

We can translate an object in Unity using a movement vector like this:

```
myObject.transform.Translate(myMovementVector);
```

The movement vector is the amount of space in a certain direction that we want the object to traverse. We want the object to traverse a fraction of the space that divides it from the goal every time interval, but how can we calculate how much space should the object traverse for, let's say, every second?

In Physics, the average space traversed by an object in a time interval moving at a certain speed is called Δs (delta space), and it's described by the following formula:

$$\Delta s = v_m * \Delta t$$

where vm is the average speed at which the object is moving and Δt is the amount of time in which the object moved of a quantity Δs (that we want to calculate).

So if our movement vector is Δs, to calculate it, we just need to multiply the average speed to the time interval.

The **speed** at which we want to move our object is an arbitrary quantity that we can make up. I will choose a value of 1, meaning that the object will move at 1 unit per second.

For the time interval Δt, we have a value provided to us by Unity that already has this information ready. This is Time.deltaTime, which is the difference between the last frame's frametime and the current frame's frametime.

Note   Frametime is the time it takes for a frame to be rendered. It's a floating value and can be different frame by frame, depending on the complexity of the scene to be rendered. Of course, an inconstant average frametime value (meaning the average between all the frametimes for every frame) is a symptom of bad performances, since it may cause stuttering, ruining the experience for the player.

`Time.deltaTime` is expressed in seconds; this means that it also helps us represent the movement as the amount of space traversed per second at speed vm.

We can use this concept for our movement vector like this:

```
myObject.transform.Translate(0, 0, speed * Time.deltaTime);
```

We applied to transform.Translate a vector [0, 0, speed * Time. deltaTime] because we want the object to be moved forward.

We need just one bit! Since we are moving our object forward, we also need to make it turn toward the new position. To do that, Unity gives us a very handy function packed in the transform class: LookAt. We can use LookAt very easily, like this:

```
this.transform.LookAt(positionToLookAt);
```

where positionToLookAt is a Vector3 representing the point in space we want the object to turn toward.

Let's see how we can apply those new information to our code:

```
1.    using UnityEngine;
2.    using System.Collections;
3.
4.    public class Move : MonoBehaviour
5.    {
6.        Vector3 goal;
```

```
7.          float speed = 1.0f;
8.          float accuracy = 1.0f;
9.
10.         void Start()
11.         {
12.             goal = this.transform.position;
13.         }
14.
15.         void Update()
16.         {
17.             RaycastHit hit;
18.             Ray ray = Camera.main.ScreenPointToRay(Input.
                mousePosition);
19.
20.             if(Physics.Raycast(ray, out hit) && Input.
                GetMouseButtonDown(0))
21.             {
22.                 goal = new Vector3(hit.point.x, this.
                    transform.position.y, hit.point.z);
23.             }
24.
25.             this.transform.LookAt(goal);
26.             if(Vector3.Distance(transform.position, goal) >
                accuracy)
27.             {
28.                 this.transform.Translate(0,0, speed*Time.
                    deltaTime);
29.             }
30.         }
31.     }
```

At **lines 6–8**, we define the variables we will use later in the code to define the goal position, the movement speed, and the accuracy. The accuracy is an offset value that we need to avoid the object to constantly do infinitesimal movement and instead use a more approximation-based movement. This means that if the object is close enough to that point, it will stop and the accuracy of this approximation is represented by the accuracy variable.

We restored the Start method, and we are using it to initialize the goal vector, which at the beginning stores the current position of the object (**lines 10–13**).

We already saw that we need to create the hit and ray variables (**lines 17–18**) to be used in the Physics.Raycast method (**line 20**). When the left mouse button is clicked, we are going to set the goal 3D vector with the coordinates taken from the hit variable, but keeping the current y coordinate (**lines 20–23**).

At **line 25**, we turn the object to face the new position we want to reach, and if the distance between the object and the goal is greater than the accuracy value we set (**line 26**), we use the Translate method to move the object toward the goal at the speed we defined (**line 28**).

Save the code and press the play button to test it! Now, when you click a point on the 3D plane, the cube will move little by little (depending on the speed you set) toward that point you clicked.

Here you are, you just created your first NPC walking toward a point!

We want to go one step further by making our cube rotate toward the goal gradually, just as we did with the actual movement. This concept is called *steering*, and it's very much used in games to simulate the natural rotation of an object. Let's see how it works!

2.2.4 Steering Behaviors

Steering behaviors are very important for nearly every kind of game and especially for simulation games like car games, and they are commonly implemented using the concept of linear interpolation. Without going too deep in the maths, linear interpolation between two points A and B calculates the points that take us from point A to point B. This concept can be applied to traverse the space from point A to point B as well as to rotate an object from an angle α to an angle β.

There are two very popular techniques to implement linear interpolation to rotate an object:

- Lerp (Linear intERPolation)

- Slerp (Spherical Linear intERPolation)

The main difference between the two is that Lerp moves the object using a constant speed, while Slerp does it by using a variable speed. This variable speed is basically the effect of the object gradually accelerating after starting moving and then gradually slowing down when approaching the goal.

In Unity, we can use Slerp with the `Quaternion.Slerp` method as follows:

```
Quaternion.Slerp(startingRotation, goalRotation, rotationSpeed);
```

The function returns a fraction of the rotation needed to turn from `startingRotation` to `goalRotation` at speed `rotationSpeed`. Our `startingRotation` would be the value of the current rotation angle of the cube, while `goalRotation` must be calculated using the method `LookRotation` from the static class `Quaternion`. For example, if we want to calculate the rotation angle to turn in the direction of our goal position, we would do something like this:

```
Vector3 direction = goal - this.transform.position;
goalRotation = Quaternion.LookRotation(direction);
```

47

This all looks pretty easy, does it? Let's use it in our script!

Open up Move.cs and let's make some modifications! First, declare a float variable called rotSpeed to define the rotation speed of the object, just under the declaration of goal, speed, and accuracy:

```
float rotSpeed = 2f;
```

Then, delete the LookAt line and replace it with those two lines:

```
Vector3 direction = goal - this.transform.position;
this.transform.rotation = Quaternion.Slerp(this.transform.
rotation, Quaternion.LookRotation(direction), Time.
deltaTime*rotSpeed);
```

Here, we are declaring a direction vector that tells us the distance and direction of the goal compared to the cube's current position; then we use this information to calculate the rotation angle using the LookRotation method, and we pass this information to the Slerp method along with the current cube's rotation value and the rotation speed times delta time.

The script should now look like this:

```
1.    using UnityEngine;
2.    using System.Collections;
3.
4.    public class Move : MonoBehaviour
5.    {
6.        Vector3 goal;
7.        float speed = 1.0f;
8.        float accuracy = 0.5f;
9.        float rotSpeed = 2f;
10.
11.       void Start()
12.       {
13.           goal = this.transform.position;
```

```
14.        }
15.
16.        void Update()
17.        {
18.            RaycastHit hit;
19.            Ray ray = Camera.main.ScreenPointToRay(Input.
               mousePosition);
20.
21.            if(Physics.Raycast(ray, out hit) && Input.
               GetMouseButtonDown(0))
22.            {
23.                goal = new Vector3(hit.point.x, this.
                   transform.posilion.y, hit.point.z);
24.            }
25.
26.            Vector3 direction = goal - this.transform.
               position;
27.
28.            if (Vector3.Distance(transform.position, goal) >
               accuracy)
29.            {
30.                this.transform.rotation = Quaternion.
                   Slerp(this.transform.rotation, Quaternion.
                   LookRotation(direction), Time.deltaTime *
                   rotSpeed);
31.                this.transform.Translate(0,0, speed*Time.
                   deltaTime);
32.            }
33.        }
34.    }
```

Once again, let's save the script and press Play! You will see that now the cube will gradually rotate toward the goal point while moving forward.

Good job! You just created your very first and basic algorithm to move an object from a point A to a point B! That's an important foundation for what's coming next: pathfinding!

In the next chapter, we will learn the foundations of pathfinding to allow our little cube to find its way toward the goal even with obstacles and no obvious path.

2.3 Test Your Knowledge!

1. What is a 2D space?

2. How are points defined in a 2D space?

3. What is a 3D space?

4. How are points defined in a 3D space?

5. What is a vector?

6. What is the difference between a 2D and a 3D vector?

7. What are the possible applications of vectors in video games?

8. How does vector sum work?

9. How does vector subtraction work?

10. What is scalar multiplication? How does it work?

11. What is dot product? How does it work? How can you use it in video games?

12. What is a geometric translation? How can you use it in a video game?

13. Explain the concept of steering behavior. Why is it important?

14. How can you implement a steering behavior in Unity?

15. Analyze the code we just wrote for this chapter's project and locate all the places where we used (or Unity probably used under the hood) the vector operations we just learned.

CHAPTER 3

Paths and Waypoints

In the last chapter, we saw how we can create a 3D object and make it move around and toward a specific point in the space. As you might expect, that code won't work in a complex context; for example, if you put the little cube in a maze, it will never be able to get to the goal coordinates. This kind of problem falls under the category of pathfinding, which focuses on finding optimal paths in a graph. Pathfinding can be used to solve nearly every problem as long as it's represented as a graph problem.

In this chapter, we will see how we can tackle pathfinding problems using fundamental mathematical tools called graphs and searching algorithms. We will cover the theory and the basic concepts, and then we will dive into the implementation of some of the most interesting techniques with Unity and C#.

3.1 Graphs

A **graph** is a set of **nodes** (or vertices) and **edges** used to represent **relationships** between concepts. Basically, nodes represent concepts, while edges represent the relationships that connect those concepts. Those relationships can be one-way or bidirectional. When a graph is made by one-way edges, it's said to be **directed**, while when it's made of bidirectional edges, it's said to be **undirected** (Figure 3-1).

© Sebastiano M. Cossu 2021
S. M. Cossu, *Beginning Game AI with Unity*,
https://doi.org/10.1007/978-1-4842-6355-6_3

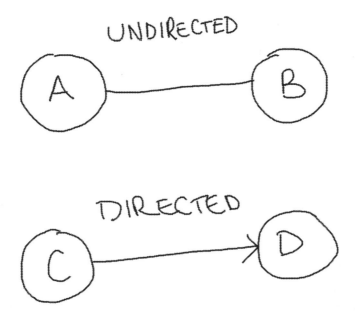

Figure 3-1. *A comparison between an undirected and a directed graph*

The easiest example we can think of is a map, where nodes represent places and edges represent streets. For example, in Figure 3-2, you can see a map of the major train routes in Great Britain, where nodes are stations and edges are rails connecting stations to each other.

The edges of the map in Figure 3-2 represent the verb `is-connected-to`. For example, the relationship between London and Dover in Figure 3-2 can be expressed as London `is-connected-to` Dover.

Figure 3-2. *The map of the major railways in Britain is an undirected graph*

The map of Britain's train routes is an undirected graph. In fact, the stations are connected in both ways, which means that you can travel from London to Dover and all the way back from Dover to London.

Roads and rails are not the only thing you can model with a graph. For example, a family tree is a directed graph that describes the parental relationships between people in the same family. In this case, the concept that the edges are representing is *generated*. In Figure 3-3, you can see a part of my family tree as an example. The edges connecting me to my parents can be expressed as Dad *generated* Me and Mom *generated* Me. The difference between a directed and an undirected graph is that connections are one-way, so they cannot be traversed in reversed order.

Figure 3-3. *A family tree is a directed graph*

The most important concept that you have to keep in mind is that every problem modeled as a graph can be solved by finding a path in that graph.

For example, let's pick Figure 3-2 again (the British Railway). Let's say you have a friend in Edinburgh, and you've just arrived in London. You want to see that friend of yours, and so you decide to take a train. What's the path you should take to get from London to Edinburgh? To answer your question, you take a look at the map and find out that there are many paths you can take, and the shortest path is traveling to York, then Newcastle, and then finally Edinburgh. So here you are! You found a path in the graph, and you solved the problem! But how can we teach an NPC to do the same?

So now that we know what a graph is, let's see how we can use it to represent a map and then we will find out how we can program an NPC to intelligently traverse that map to reach an arbitrarily chosen point.

3.2 Waypoints

The traditional way to represent places and coordinates in space is using **waypoints**. Waypoints are points on a line of travel that mark specific locations. It may be to mark important landmarks, changes in the main route, and so on. They are used by all the navigation systems from cartography to GPS-based navigation systems and even the most simple kind of maps, like treasure maps (Figure 3-4).

It's very easy to apply graph searching algorithms to a waypoint system because they are in fact graphs! That's why our first implementation of a pathfinding algorithm will be based on a waypoint system. It's not currently the most used way to create maps in games, but it's a very interesting starting point as it can help you understand better how more complex or modern technologies work under the hood and how graphs and search algorithms really work.

Figure 3-4. *Waypoints are widely used in cartography, even in very simple maps*

3.2.1 A Simple Path

Let's start with something simple! We will build a path made of waypoints and instruct our agent to walk through it.

Create a new 3D project, and in the default scene, right-click the Hierarchy and select Create ➤ 3D Object ➤ Plane and position the plane at the coordinate X = 10, Y= 0, Z = 0 with a scale value of 10 for all the axis, as shown in Figure 3-5.

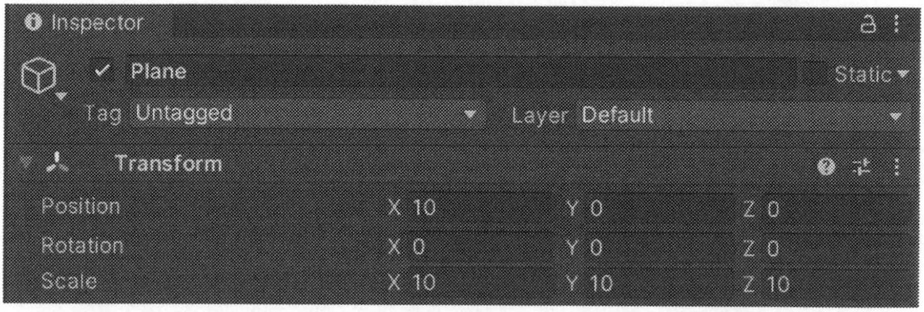

Figure 3-5. *The coordinate and scale values of the plane*

Now we need to create some more objects. To start, we will create the object that will represent our agent. So right-click again the Hierarchy window and select Create ➤ 3D Object ➤ Cube and rename it Agent and position it anywhere in the plane; the only important thing is that it's placed just upon the plane, so that it will seem like it's moving on the plane. You can use the setting in Figure 3-6 as a reference.

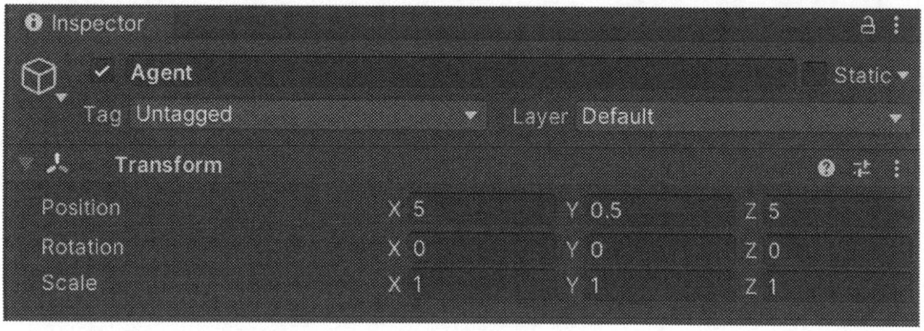

Figure 3-6. *The coordinate and scale values of the agent*

Now we need to create the actual waypoints that will mark the path our agent will follow.

We are going to make the waypoints with simple 3D spheres, so let's create some 3D spheres by right-clicking the Hierarchy and selecting 3D Object ➤ Sphere. Place the spheres in the order you like. For example, in Figure 3-7, you can see that I placed them in a circle.

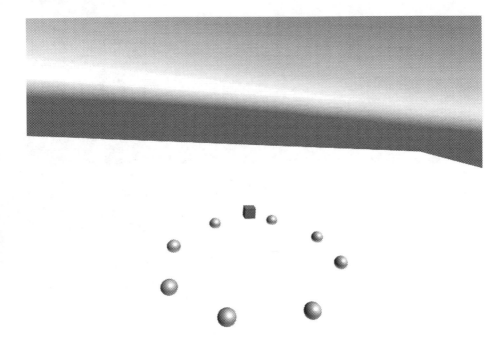

Figure 3-7. *The waypoints are creating a circle path*

Now we have all set and we only need to create the code to make the agent walk the waypoints path.

The plan is to create an array that contains all the waypoints and loop through them to allow the agent to walk toward them one by one in the order they are sorted in the array. Once the agent reaches the last waypoint, it starts over from the first one. We will implement the agent's movements using what we learned in Chapter 2.

Create a new C# script (right-click the Assets panel ➤ Create ➤ C# Script), rename it *WalkWP.cs*, and assign it to the Agent object (the cube); you can do it by simply dragging and dropping the script onto the Game Object. As usual, I will show you the code, and then I will explain every line and the overall logic.

```
1.    using System.Collections;
2.    using System.Collections.Generic;
3.    using UnityEngine;
4.
5.    public class WalkWP : MonoBehaviour
6.    {
7.            public GameObject[] path;
8.            private Vector3 goal;
9.            private float speed = 4.0f;
10.       private float accuracy = 0.5f;
11.       private float rotSpeed = 4f;
12.       private int curNode = 0;
13.
14.       void Update()
15.       {
16.           goal = new Vector3(path[curNode].transform.
              position.x,
17.                                this.transform.position.y,
                                  path[curNode].transform.
                                  position.z);
18.           Vector3 direction = goal - this.transform.
              position;
19.
20.           if (direction.magnitude > accuracy)
21.           {
```

```
22.                 this.transform.rotation = Quaternion.Slerp
                    (this.transform.rotation, Quaternion.
                    LookRotation(direction), Time.deltaTime *
                    rotSpeed);
23.                 this.transform.Translate(0, 0, speed * Time.
                    deltaTime);
24.             }
25.         else
26.         {
27.             if (curNode < path.Length - 1)
28.             {
29.                 curNode++;
30.             }
31.             else
32.             {
33.                 curNode = 0;
34.             }
35.         }
36.     }
37. }
```

At **line 7**, we declare an array to hold the waypoints so that we can loop through them. Declaring it as a public variable will allow us to populate it from the Inspector.

At **line 9**, we declare the variable that will contain the current goal that the agent will need to reach. This goal will be updated with the next waypoint in the path array every time the agent reaches the current goal.

At **lines 10–12**, we declare and set the values related to the movements of the agent like its movement speed (line 10), its rotation speed (line 12), and the accuracy (line 11) which is the distance at which the agent will stop from the goal.

At **line 13**, we declare curNode which will hold the index in the array path that points to the current waypoint we are considering as the current goal for the agent.

Inside the Update function, there is all the logic we need to make use of our waypoint path.

At **line 17**, we update the goal with the current waypoint we are taking from the path array, while at **line 18** we set the agent's direction to point toward the new goal.

At **line 21**, we check if the agent is close enough to the goal according to the accuracy value, and in case it is not, we rotate the agent to face the goal (line 23), and then we move it forward by the value of speed (line 24).

From **lines 21** to **36**, there is the logic to update the array index that points to the current waypoint in the path array. If the agent is close enough to the goal, we want to update the index instead, so in the next iteration we can update the goal with the next waypoint. So, as we said, we check if the value of the index curNode is still inside the array's bound (line 28), and in case it is, we increase it by one (line 30) so in the next iteration we can set the goal to the next waypoint in the path; otherwise, we set the index to zero, so we can start over from the first waypoint in the array.

Now go back to the Unity Editor and select the object Agent from the Hierarchy, and in the Inspector, you will see the path array we just created in the script file as shown in Figure 3-8.

Figure 3-8. *The path array is empty (size = 0)*

To populate the array, you need to drag and drop the Waypoints Game Objects (the spheres) on the array name in the Inspector. To do that, you have to select the object Agent and lock its Inspector page, so it doesn't get replaced when you select another object. To lock an Inspector page, you can click the little padlock on the heading of the Inspector tab. Once clicked, the padlock icon will become a closed padlock (Figure 3-9). You can unlock it again by clicking the padlock again.

Figure 3-9. *The padlock is closed; it means that the current Inspector page won't be replaced when selecting another object*

After locking the Inspector page, select all the waypoints objects (the spheres) from either the Hierarchy or the 3D scene window, drag them, and drop them on the path array in the Inspector to populate it with them (Figure 3-10).

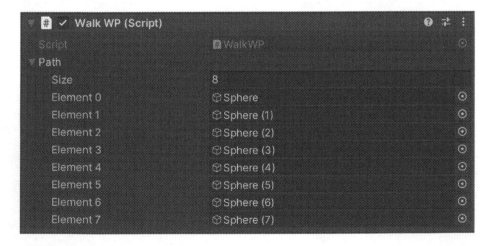

Figure 3-10. *The path array is now populated with all the waypoints*

Now that everything is set, we only need to test it. Save and run the game! You will see the Agent walking around following one by one all the waypoints. Now that you have all the logic working correctly, you can rearrange the position of the waypoints to make different paths for the agent to follow.

3.2.2 A Labyrinth!

We saw how to create a waypoint system to build a path so that an Agent can move around following the points. We will now make the next step and create something more complex. We will represent the 3D space using the principle of board games: dividing the 3D space in a grid where every tile is a waypoint. Just like in a boardgame like Draughts (Figure 3-11), our agent will be only able to move between those waypoints/tiles. A tile can be walkable or non-walkable, depending on the rules of our game; our objective is to teach the agent how to move around the maze and reach the goal – which will be a tile specified by us.

Figure 3-11. *A Draughts' board. Boards in board games can be easily represented as graphs*

Note   Using a grid is not the only way to make a waypoint system or the best one. It's just one of the ways to do it, and I personally think it's one of the easiest and more straightforward, which is crucial for learning purposes. The best way to represent your world with a waypoint system depends on what you need to do in your game or application. Software engineering is not about absolute answers or learning formulas by heart, it's about the use of scientific principles to design and implement appropriate solutions to problems.

In code, this will be represented as a 2D matrix where every element is a waypoint. We will store the information related to every waypoint by implementing a custom class called Node (remember that waypoints represent the same concept as nodes).

Let's start by creating a new 3D project, and in the default scene, let's modify the point of view of the Main Camera object. We want it to directly face the floor so that we can see the scene from the top. To do that, select the Main Camera from the Hierarchy window and change its Position in the Inspector to X = 15, Y = 35, Z = 15, and its Rotation to X = 90, Y = 0, Z = 0.

Create a 3D project and create a new 3D plane in the scene by right-clicking the Hierarchy window and selecting 3D Object ➤ Plane.

Select the newly created plane and change its Position in the Inspector to be X = 10, Y = 0, Z = 0 and its Scale to X = 10, Y = 10, Z = 10 as shown in Figure 3-12. This is just a static blank plane to serve aesthetically as a base of the map.

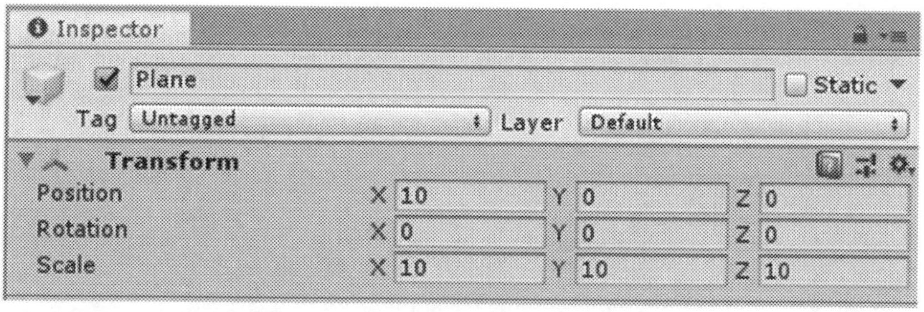

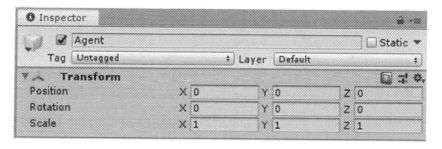

Figure 3-12. *The properties of the Plane object as seen in the Inspector*

Now create a new object for the agent by right-clicking the Hierarchy window and selecting 3D Object ➤ Cube. Call this cube "Agent" and change its Position to X = 0, Y = 0, Z = 0 (Figure 3-13).

Figure 3-13. *The properties of the object Agent as seen in the Inspector*

Finally, we need to create the object that will graphically represent a waypoint in the 3D world. Of course visual representation is not needed as long as we have the coordinates of the points, but to visualize what is happening on the screen makes it easier for us to understand what is happening. So create a new plane by right-clicking the Hierarchy window and selecting 3D Object ➤ Plane and call it *Waypoint*. Then, just change its Position property to X = 0, Y = 0, Z = 0 and its Scale values to X = 0.4, Y = 1, and Z = 0.4 as shown in Figure 3-14.

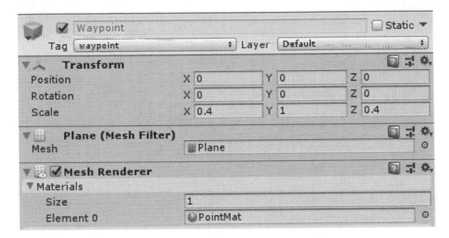

Figure 3-14. *The properties of the Waypoint object as seen in the Inspector*

Now drag the Waypoint object and drop it in the Assets window. This action will turn the object into a prefab, which is a reusable object. We will need it as a prefab to generate all the waypoints for the map. You can now delete the object from the Hierarchy window, since we have it now in the Assets window.

We will also need different materials to apply to the waypoints to mark them as walkable or nonwalkable and to mark the point that is also the final goal. So create three Materials of three different colors by right-clicking the Assets window and selecting Create ➤ Material and changing their color value in the Inspector window. Call them GoalMat, PointMat, and WallMat. The default material for the waypoint should be PointMat, so drag and drop it on the object Waypoint; this action will apply the material to the prefab.

OK, now that the scene and objects are set up, we can concentrate on the code. Right-click the Assets window and select Create ➤ C# Script, call the new script GridWP.cs, and double-click it to open it up in your favorite editor.

As we said, we need a Node class to represent waypoints, and we can create it just here, inside GridWP.cs, so let's do it!

```
1.    public class GridWP : MonoBehaviour
2.    {
3.
4.        public class Node
5.        {
6.            private int depth;
7.            private bool walkable;
8.
9.            private GameObject waypoint = new GameObject();
10.           private List<Node> neighbors = new List<Node>();
11.
12.           public int Depth { get => depth; set => depth =
                  value; }
13.           public bool Walkable { get => walkable; set =>
                  walkable = value; }
14.
15.           public GameObject Waypoint { get => waypoint; set
                  => waypoint = value; }
16.           public List<Node> Neighbors { get => neighbors;
                  set => neighbors = value; }
17.
18.           public Node()
19.           {
20.               this.depth = -1;
21.               this.walkable = true;
22.           }
23.
24.           public Node(bool walkable)
25.           {
```

```
26.                     this.depth = -1;
27.                     this.walkable = walkable;
28.                 }
29.
30.             public override bool Equals(System.Object obj)
31.                 {
32.                     if (obj == null) return false;
33.                     Node n = obj as Node;
34.                     if ((System.Object)n == null)
35.                     {
36.                         return false;
37.                     }
38.                     if (this.waypoint.transform.position.x ==
                        n.Waypoint.transform.position.x &&
39.                         this.waypoint.transform.position.z ==
                            n.Waypoint.transform.position.z)
40.                     {
41.                         return true;
42.                     }
43.                     return false;
44.                 }
45.         }
46.     }
```

At **line 6**, we are declaring a variable that represents the depth of the current node in relation to the position in the graph of the starting node. We will use this information in the implementation of the graph search algorithm to reconstruct the shortest path.

At **line 7**, we are declaring the walkable variable that will tell us if the node is walkable.

At **line 9**, we declare a `GameObject` variable that will be used to store the instance of the `Waypoint prefab` we created in the `Unity Editor`. The reference to that `GameObject` will allow us to easily do things like apply materials on waypoints based on their characteristics and get the coordinates in the 3D space.

At **line 10**, we declare a `List` of `Nodes` that will contain references to all the nodes that are **neighbors** of the current node. With the word neighbor, I mean any node directly connected to the current node. In this case, nodes represent tiles in a grid, and they are connected if they are adjacent in the grid in one of the four basic directions: up, down, left, right; we are not considering diagonal movements.

Lines 12–16 are just the getters and setters of the class properties defined in **lines 4–8**.

In **lines 18–22**, we define the basic class constructor method that takes zero parameters and sets the properties with their predefined values. We set `depth` by default to a negative value (line 21) because it's a kind of value that we cannot obtain when we will run the algorithm, as the distance between the goal node and the starting node can only be a positive value. We also set the `walkable` property to true as we want new nodes to be walkable by default (line 22).

At **lines 24–28**, we define another constructor to quickly set a node as unwalkable just during the creation. The only thing that changes between this constructor and the previous one is that this takes a boolean parameter (line 26) to initialize the `walkable` property (line 29).

At **lines 30–44**, we override the Equal method for the Node class, to define our own way to compare nodes. In fact, Equal is the method used to compare two objects that are instances of the same class; by overriding it, we can redefine the way they should be compared. In this case, we say two Nodes are equivalent if the waypoints they contain share the same X and Z coordinates. We will use this method in the search algorithm to check if we reached the goal node.

Now that we have the Node class, we need some more variables to be declared as GridWP's properties. Let's list them and describe them very quickly:

```
1.   public Node[,] grid;
2.   List<Node> path = new List<Node>();
3.   int curNode = 0;
4.
5.   public GameObject prefabWaypoint;
6.   public Material goalMat;
7.   public Material wallMat;
8.
9.   Vector3 goal;
10.  float speed = 4.0f;
11.  float accuracy = 0.5f;
12.  float rotSpeed = 4f;
13.
14.  int spacing = 5;
15.
16.  Node startNode;
17.  Node endNode;
```

At **line 1**, we define the matrix that we will use to store all our waypoints. This matrix will represent the space as a tiled board in a board game, as we said in the previous section.

At **line 2**, we declare a list of nodes that we will use to represent the final path that the agent will walk by reaching every waypoint/node in the list. The list will be traversed using the counter defined at line 3.

At **lines 5–7**, we declare public fields that will contain our Waypoint prefab and the different materials representing the goal and the nonwalkable nodes, while at **line 14** we define an integer variable that we will use as an offset to put some space between the points in the 3D scene.

For each node, we will create an instance of the Waypoint prefab so that the node can be represented visually in the 3D space.

At **lines 9–12**, we declare some of the variables that we already saw in the previous section. Those variables are goal, speed, accuracy, and rotSpeed, and they will be useful to implement the actual movement of the agent in the 3D space. The principle of how the agent will move toward an objective point will be the same, but the logic will be a bit different as we have a list of points that make the path and not just a single node. The goal will be set the first time to the first node of the path list, and it will change to the next one in the list when the agent will reach it.

Finally, at **lines 16** and **17**, we define two containers in which we will put the references to the starting and final nodes.

OK, we finished declaring variables; now we can concentrate on the actual functionality by implementing some methods.

As we said, for every node, we will need the list of its adjacent nodes and store it in the neighbors property. So let's write a method to calculate this list. We assume that we will receive a reference to the matrix containing all the nodes and the coordinates to the matrix for the current node of which we want to calculate the adjacent nodes.

The adjacent nodes will be calculated only considering the four basic directions: up, down, left, right – this means that we will have at most four adjacent nodes.

To obtain the adjacent nodes in a 2D matrix in the way I just explained, we will need to add or subtract 1 to the row and column numbers. For example, given a matrix called M, we can get the neighbors of an element at coordinates M[r,c] (where r is the row number and c is the column number) like this:

```
Up: M[r-1, c]
Right: M[r, c+1]
Down: M[r+1, c]
Left: M[r, c-1]
```

Now that we have a strategy, let's write up the code for the method. This will be placed inside the GridWP class, but outside the Node class:

```
1.          List<Node> getAdjacentNodes(Node[,] m, int i, int j)
2.          {
3.              List<Node> l = new List<Node>();
4.
5.              // node up
6.              if (i-1 >= 0)
7.                  if (m[i-1, j].Walkable)
8.                  {
9.                      l.Add(m[i - 1, j]);
10.                 }
11.
12.             // node down
13.             if (i+1 < m.GetLength(0))
14.                 if (m[i + 1, j].Walkable)
15.                 {
16.                     l.Add(m[i + 1, j]);
17.                 }
18.
19.             // node left
20.             if (j-1 >= 0)
21.                 if (m[i, j - 1].Walkable)
22.                 {
23.                     l.Add(m[i, j-1]);
24.                 }
25.
26.             // node right
27.             if (j+1 < m.GetLength(1))
28.                 if (m[i, j + 1].Walkable)
29.                 {
```

```
30.                    l.Add(m[i, j+1]);
31.                }
32.
33.            return l;
34.        }
```

In the signature, we declare that this method returns a list of nodes representing the list of the adjacent nodes and takes three parameters: the matrix labeled m and the coordinates in the matrix for the node of which we want to calculate the neighbors labeled i and j (line 1).

At **line 3**, we start by creating a temporary list to contain the neighbors, and we call it l.

The first thing we need to do before picking the nodes is to check if the indexes of the neighbor nodes are going out of the bounds of the matrix. In fact, for example, we cannot ask the matrix for the element M[-1][c], as the indexes of a matrix can only be positive values, so we need to check, before accessing the matrix, if the indexes are valid or not, and we do it in **lines 6**, **13**, **20**, and **27**.

After checking if the indexes are valid, we check if the current node was marked as walkable, because if it's not walkable, it means that it's not connected to the current node – in fact, as we said previously, nodes in a graph are connected only if they are related, and in this case, the relation means that there is a path between two nodes, so if one of the two nodes is not walkable, there cannot be a path; hence, it's not a neighbor. We check that in **lines 7**, **14**, **21**, and **28** for all the four directions (if the previous check succeeded).

Finally, if both the checks succeeded, we add the nodes to the list at **lines 9**, **16**, **23**, and **30** and return the list at **line 33**.

Now that all the properties and functionalities related to node representations are done, we need to initialize the matrix that will contain our waypoints. We will do this in the Start method. What we need to do is to initialize the matrix containing all the nodes and then loop into the matrix to initialize the GameObjects inside the nodes and calculate the list of the adjacent nodes for each of them. Finally, we will set one of the nodes to be the goal, and we position the agent to the starting point. So let's write up our Start method:

```
1.      void Start()
2.   {
3.       // create grid
4.       grid = new Node[,] {
5.           { new Node(),        new Node(),        new Node(false),
                 new Node(),      new Node(), new Node() },
6.           { new Node(),        new Node(false),   new Node(),
                 new Node(),      new Node(), new Node() },
7.           { new Node(),        new Node(false),   new Node(),
                 new Node(), new Node(), new Node() },
8.           { new Node(),        new Node(),        new Node(),
                 new Node(false), new Node(), new Node() },
9.           { new Node(),        new Node(),        new Node(),
                 new Node(),      new Node(false), new Node() },
10.          { new Node(),        new Node(),        new Node(false),
                 new Node(),      new Node(false), new Node() },
11.          { new Node(),        new Node(false),   new Node(false),
                 new Node(),      new Node(), new Node() }
12.      };
13.
14.      // initialize grid points
15.      for (int i = 0; i < grid.GetLength(0); i++)
16.      {
17.          for (int j = 0; j < grid.GetLength(1); j++)
18.          {
19.              grid[i, j].Waypoint = Instantiate(prefabWaypoint,
                     new Vector3(i * spacing, this.transform.position.y,
                     j * spacing), Quaternion.identity);
```

```
20.
21.            if (!grid[i, j].Walkable)
22.            {
23.                grid[i, j].Waypoint.GetComponent
                   <Renderer>().material = wallMat;
24.            }
25.            else
26.            {
27.                grid[i, j].Neighbors = getAdjacentNodes
                   (grid, i, j);
28.            }
29.         }
30.      }
31.
32.      startNode = grid[0, 0];
33.      endNode = grid[6, 5];
34.      startNode.Walkable = true;
35.      endNode.Walkable = true;
36.      endNode.Waypoint.GetComponent<Renderer>().material =
         goalMat;
37.
38.      this.transform.position = new Vector3(startNode.
         Waypoint.transform.position.x, this.transform.
         position.y, startNode.Waypoint.transform.position.z);
39.   }
```

At **lines 4–12**, we initialize the matrix called grid with an arbitrary number of nodes. In this stage, we only decide the ones that will be walkable and the ones that won't by using the Node class' initializer.

In **lines 15–30**, we loop through the matrix, and as we do, we create an instance of `prefabWaypoint` and associate it to the current node which is stored inside the matrix at the current coordinates (line 19).

At **lines 21–28**, we check if the node is walkable: if it is, we calculate the adjacent nodes and store them in the neighbors list (line 27); if it's not, we set the `wallMat` material to the `prefabWaypoint` we just associated to the node (line 23).

Once we have initialized the grid and all the nodes, we set the starting and final nodes at **lines 32–33**; we make sure both are walkable at **lines 34–36**, and we apply the `goalMat` material to endNode's associated `prefabWaypoint` instance.

Finally, we set the agent's position to an arbitrary starting point at **line 38**.

Now that the grid is set up, we can take a look at how it looks. Go back to the `Unity Editor` and drag and drop the `GridWP` script on the `Agent` in the `Hierarchy` window.

Now selecting the `Agent` by left-clicking it in the `Hierarchy` window, you will see the script attached and the public fields we just created: `Prefab Waypoint`, `Goal Mat`, and `Wall Mat`. Drag the `Waypoint prefab` from the `Assets` window and drop it on the `Prefab Point` field in the `GridWP` script in the `Inspector`. Then drag the `GoalMat` material and drop it on the `Goal Mat` field. Finally, drag the `WallMat` material and drop it on the `Wall Mat` field.

Now the script is set and you can press the `Play` button! The grid we just created in the code will be rendered on the screen with the walkable, unwalkable, and goal tiles highlighted with the correct material as shown in Figure 3-15.

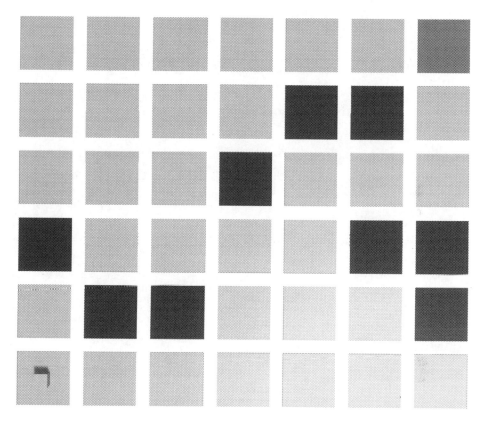

Figure 3-15. *The grid represented physically in the 3D scene with the different materials marking the different characteristics of the waypoints/tiles*

To conclude the general setup of the script and start talking about pathfinding algorithms, we just need to add the functionality to let the Agent walk around and move toward the nodes in the path list one by one. This part of the code will be very similar to what we already made for the simpler waypoints example in the previous section.

We can implement this functionality in the Update method as we want those decisions to be taken constantly in the game. So, as usual, let's take a look at the code and explain what it does:

```
1.    void LateUpdate()
2.    {
3.        // calculate the shortest path when the return key is
              pressed
4.        if (Input.GetKeyDown(KeyCode.Return))
5.        {
6.            this.transform.position = new Vector3(startNode.
                  Waypoint.transform.position.x, this.transform.
                  position.y, startNode.Waypoint.transform.position.z);
7.            curNode = 0;
8.            path.add(grid[0,1]);
9.            path.add(endNode);
10.       }
11.
12.       // if there's no path, do nothing
13.       if (path.Count == 0) return;
14.
15.       // set the goal position
16.       goal = new Vector3(path[curNode].Waypoint.transform.
              position.x, this.transform.position.y, path[curNode].
              Waypoint.transform.position.z);
17.
18.       // set the direction
19.       Vector3 direction = goal - this.transform.position;
20.
21.       // move toward the goal or increase the counter to
              set another goal in the next iteration
22.       if (direction.magnitude > accuracy)
23.       {
24.           this.transform.rotation = Quaternion.
                  Slerp(this.transform.rotation, Quaternion.
```

```
                 LookRotation(direction), Time.deltaTime *
                 rotSpeed);
25.              this.transform.Translate(0, 0, speed * Time.
                 deltaTime);
26.          }
27.      else
28.          {
29.              if (curNode < path.Count - 1)
30.              {
31.                  curNode++;
32.              }
33.          }
34.  }
```

When the user presses the enter key (line 4), the code resets the position of the Agent to the start position of the grid (line 6), resets the curNode variable to 0 (line 7), and adds a couple of arbitrary chosen nodes to the path variable (lines 8–9). This is just for testing purposes, to see that everything is working fine, and we can start implementing an algorithm that returns a path as a list of nodes and be sure that it will be correctly interpreted by the Agent.

At **line 13**, we check if the path is empty, and if it is, we do nothing and just return from the method. If the path is not empty, we set the first goal to the first node in the list (line 16), and like we did in the previous chapter, we set the direction (line 19), and then if the Agent hasn't reached the goal yet, we move it toward it (lines 22–26); otherwise, we increase the curNode counter so that in the next iteration the goal will be set to the next node in the list (lines 27–33).

Save the script and run the game by pressing the Play button. The grid will be created as usual, and as soon as you press the enter button, the agent will start moving toward the point in grid[0,1] and then toward the endNode.

OK, we have our waypoint system! Now we can start talking about algorithms; we will start with one of the most famous and important algorithms: **Breadth-First Search**.

3.3 Breadth-First Search

Breadth-First Search (BFS) is one of the most important graph searching algorithms upon which a lot of more complex and widely used algorithms build.

BFS guarantees to always find the **shortest path** connecting two given nodes in a graph, if a path exists. Sounds like a very useful algorithm, right? Let's see how it works with an example!

Let's say you want to make a rock band, and you need someone that can play the drums. You will ask your friends if one of them does play drums, and if none of them do, you will probably ask them to let you know if they know someone that does. Your friends will probably do the same: they will ask their friends and then ask them to check their friends too. We can definitely model this problem with a graph!

Figure 3-16. *A group of friends is a graph too!*

In Figure 3-16, you can see a group of friends modeled as a graph whose edges represent the verb *is-friend-with*. For convenience, you prefer not to go too deep in that network because it's better to play with someone that's more close to you and to the people you trust than a total stranger. So if you want to find a person in that network that plays the drums, you need to check all your friends one by one (first-level connections) to see if they play drums; if they don't, you go one level deeper and check their friends one by one; if none of their friends do play drums, you go deeper and check the friends of your friends; and so on. If you will be successful in your search, you will eventually end up with a connection to the person that plays drums.

If we represent this network of friends as a graph, the connection between you and the person that plays drums is a path connecting two nodes in a graph, and if the final node (the drummer) is also the closest friend you can have in that network, that path is also the shortest one (Figure 3-17).

Figure 3-17. *We can solve the problem of finding a drummer by applying BFS to a group of friends*

By searching a drummer for your band, you applied Breadth-First Search (BFS). In BFS, you start from a specific node, and the first thing is to check that it's not the node you're looking for, finally you check all its adjacent nodes. If you don't find what you are looking for in the adjacent nodes, you check all the adjacent nodes of the nodes you just checked... and so on. To recreate the path connecting the starting point to the goal point, you just go backward from the goal node and look for the neighbors to reconstruct the shortest path. Remember that we added a depth property to the nodes that will be set to a value representing the depth at which we discovered that node traversing the graph from the starting position. We will use that value to decide which one of the neighbors is part of the shortest path.

Let's start by writing the signature of the method:

```
List<Node> BFS(Node start, Node end)
```

The BFS method takes as parameters the start and end nodes and returns a list of nodes that is the final path connecting the starting node to the goal node.

To implement BFS, we need to keep track of all the nodes we want to visit and all the nodes that we already visited so that we don't check a node twice. So we need two data structures.

Since BFS checks all the neighbors first and then goes deeper and checks all the neighbors of the neighbors, the nodes that are added last to the collection of the nodes to visit must be visited last. This means that for the collection of the nodes we need to visit, it's more convenient to have a FIFO (First In First Out) data structure. We will implement this with a **queue**.

For what concerns the collection of visited nodes, we can go with any collection that takes a constant or linear time to check if a specific node is contained. In fact, we will need this collection only to check if we already visited a node to make sure we are not checking things twice. Because of those necessities, I decided to go with a **list**.

Those are the only considerations we have to do for the implementation, since we already talked about the logic of the algorithm, so let's take a look at the complete code for the BFS.

```
1.    List<Node> BFS(Node start, Node end)
2.    {
3.        Queue<Node> toVisit = new Queue<Node>();
4.        List<Node> visited = new List<Node>();
5.
6.        Node currentNode = start;
7.        currentNode.Depth = 0;
8.        toVisit.Enqueue(currentNode);
9.
10.       List<Node> finalPath = new List<Node>();
11.
12.       while(toVisit.Count > 0)
13.       {
```

```
14.          currentNode = toVisit.Dequeue();
15.
16.          if (visited.Contains(currentNode))
17.              continue;
18.
19.          visited.Add(currentNode);
20.
21.          if (currentNode.Equals(end))
22.          {
23.              while (currentNode.Depth != 0)
24.              {
25.                  foreach(Node n in currentNode.Neighbors)
26.                  {
27.                      if (n.Depth == currentNode.Depth-1)
28.                      {
29.                          finalPath.Add(currentNode);
30.                          currentNode = n;
31.                          break;
32.                      }
33.                  }
34.              }
35.              finalPath.Reverse();
36.              break;
37.          }
38.          else
39.          {
40.              foreach (Node n in currentNode.Neighbors)
41.              {
42.                  if (!visited.Contains(n) && n.Walkable)
43.                  {
44.                      n.Depth = currentNode.Depth+1;
```

```
45.                    toVisit.Enqueue(n);
46.                 }
47.              }
48.           }
49.        }
50.     return finalPath;
51.  }
```

At **lines 3** and **4**, we declare the two data structures that we talked about in the previous paragraph: toVisit and visited. The former is the collection of all the nodes still to be visited, while the latter is the collection of all the already visited nodes.

At **lines 6–8**, we store the starting node in a temporary variable that we will use as a reference to the current node to visit (line 7), and then we set its depth value to 0 (since the starting node has the lowest depth value) at line 8. Then, we put the starting node in the toVisit queue so we can start the search.

At **line 10**, we initialize the path list that in the end should contain the shortest path connecting the starting node to the goal.

Lines 12–48 contain the main loop of the BFS; let's take a closer look!

Inside the main loop, we assign the next node to visit to the currentNode variable dequeuing it from the toVisit queue (line 14), and then we check if this node was already visited (lines 16–17); if it wasn't, we start the visit by adding it to the visited list (line 19).

At **line 21**, we check if the current node is also the goal node.

If the current node is not the goal (lines 39–49), we loop through all its adjacent nodes, and if they're not visited and they're walkable, we add them to the queue of nodes to visit.

If the current node is the actual goal (line 21), instead, we start a loop to find the way back to the starting node with depth 0 (line 23). For every node starting from the goal, we search through all its adjacent nodes (line 25) looking for the node with the depth value equal to currentNode.

Depth-1 (line 27) – which means it's the previous step in the shortest path. When we find that node, we put the current node into the final path, and then we set the new node we just found as the new value for currentNode (line 30), and we exit the foreach by calling a break (line 31). We repeat this process for all the nodes until we reach the starting point (meaning that currentNode.Depth will be equal to 0), and then we reverse the path and return it (lines 36–37).

Finally, if there is not a path connecting the starting node and the goal node, the algorithm just returns an empty list.

Now that the BFS is ready, we only need to use it inside the Update method, so we need to modify only the part when we generate the path after capturing the enter key pressed by the user. Let's see how the Update method should look like now:

```
1.   void LateUpdate()
2.   {
3.       // calculate the shortest path when the return key is
             pressed
4.       if (Input.GetKeyDown(KeyCode.Return))
5.       {
6.           this.transform.position = new Vector3(startNode.
               Waypoint.transform.position.x, this.transform.
               position.y, startNode.Waypoint.transform.position.z);
7.           curNode = 0;
8.           path = BFS(startNode, endNode);
9.       }
10.
11.      // if there's no path, do nothing
12.      if (path.Count == 0) return;
13.
14.      // set the goal position
```

```
15.        goal = new Vector3(path[curNode].Waypoint.transform.
           position.x,
16.                            this.transform.position.y,
17.                            path[curNode].Waypoint.transform.
                               position.z);
18.
19.        // set the direction
20.        Vector3 direction = goal - this.transform.position;
21.
22.        // move toward the goal or increase the counter to
              set another goal in the next iteration
23.        if (direction.magnitude > accuracy)
24.        {
25.            this.transform.rotation = Quaternion.
               Slerp(this.transform.rotation, Quaternion.
               LookRotation(direction), Time.deltaTime * rotSpeed);
26.            this.transform.Translate(0, 0, speed * Time.
               deltaTime);
27.        }
28.        else
29.        {
30.            if (curNode < path.Count - 1)
31.            {
32.                curNode++;
33.            }
34.        }
35.    }
```

The only line changed is **line 8** that now generates the path from the BFS algorithm. If there is a path connecting the origin and the goal, it will be stored as a list of Nodes inside the path list, and then it will be traversed by the Agent. If there is not a path connecting those two nodes, path will be empty and the Agent will stay still (line 11).

Everything is set and you can finally test your very first pathfinding algorithm based on Waypoints! Let's save the code and press Play in the Unity Editor. As soon as you press Enter, the Agent will start walking step by step through all the waypoints until it will eventually reach the goal waypoint (Figure 3-18).

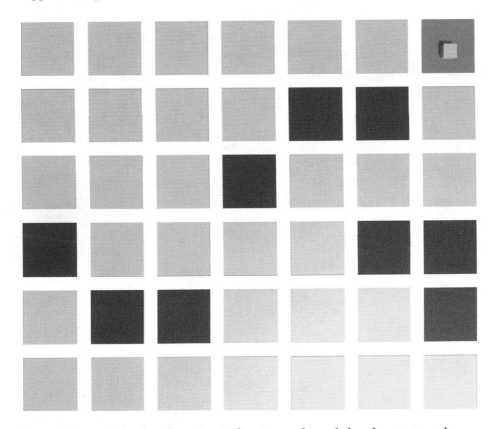

Figure 3-18. *The final project! The Agent found the shortest path toward the goal!*

Take your time to make experiments changing the size and shape of the grid and the position of the starting point and the goal and enjoy your very first intelligent agent able to find the shortest path in a maze!

In the next chapter, we will explore another technique widely used in video games to solve pathfinding problems. We will introduce the concept of NavMesh and talk about A*, the most popular pathfinding algorithm in the game industry.

3.4 Exercises

Another very important and fundamental algorithm is Depth-First Search (DFS). In this section, I will explain the theory around this algorithm, but since we have a working waypoint system in place, I will leave the C# implementation to you as an exercise.

If BFS searches for the node looking at all the possible branches in parallel, the DFS algorithm picks a way and goes down to its bottom. If the goal is not found, it goes back and tries another unvisited branch.

DFS can be very useful when you have a very deep tree; in this case, it can find the solution way before BFS. BFS performs better with very wide and not very deep trees, but the main difference is that BFS always finds the shortest path, while DFS only finds a path, not necessarily the shortest.

For obvious reasons, DFS is very often implemented as a recursive algorithm, but depending on the size of the tree and the resources available, it may be implemented as an iterative algorithm as well.

Try to implement DFS using the waypoint system created in this chapter!

CHAPTER 4

Navigation

In Chapter 2, we saw how to program the basic characteristics of a navigation agent, like steering and moving toward a goal, and in Chapter 3 we learned what a pathfinding algorithm is and how it works, and we implemented one using a waypoint system to represent the walkable area.

In this chapter, we are going to use what we learned in the previous chapters while we explore different ways to solve the navigation problem. The new methods I am going to cover in this chapter are more effective and efficient in complex scenarios. They were introduced when 3D environments in video games started to become popular, and they are still widely used in the game industry now as in the years they became the de facto standard to solve the navigation problem in 3D environments. The techniques I am talking about are best-first search algorithms and weighted graphs and in particular A* and Navigation Meshes.

4.1 Weighted Graphs

We saw in Chapter 3 how a Breadth-First Search algorithm works, by expanding all the nodes at the same level and then expanding the lower-level nodes. This balanced exploring procedure works well in many cases, but it sacrifices the space used in memory (the allocated memory to store the explored nodes might become very big before the algorithm finds the goal), and more importantly, it may take a lot of time in some cases.

Imagine the following scenario (Figure 4-1): you have a root node called A and three children called B, C, and D. D is the goal node and it's directly connected to A, so the time to reach it should be the quickest possible. Unfortunately, if we use Breadth-First Search, we will find the path A→D only after checking A→B and A→C, which is three times the amount of time we should have spent to find A→D in the first place. This problem becomes even worse if B, C, and D have children, and the solution is two or three levels deep in D's branch.

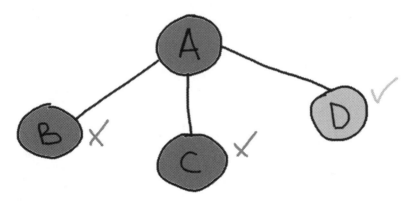

Figure 4-1. *A very simple graph that shows the kind of scenario where BFS might fall short*

The problem of wasting time and resources to find the path to a goal node is clearly an important one and crucial in AI research, and there is still no perfect solution to that problem, and in complex situation with very big graphs, it's still a challenge to find the path to a goal in a reasonable amount of time and resources wise. The only approach that is really helping a lot with that is the use of best-first search in weighted graphs using a good heuristic function. What does it mean? Let's find out!

A weighted graph is a graph where walking to a node has a cost, and this cost differs between different nodes. A path connecting two nodes has a cost X, where X is the sum of the costs of all the nodes that connect the two nodes. In the example in Figure 4-2, the path ABEG connecting A to G has a cost of 1+2+1 = 4. ABEG is also the shortest path; in fact, the only other path that connects A to G is ACEG which has a cost of 2+2+1 = 5.

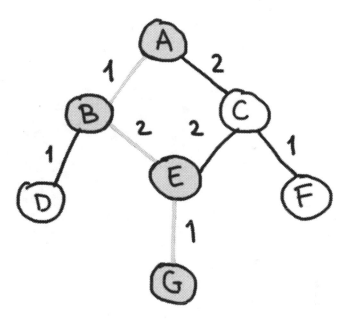

Figure 4-2. *A weighted graph*

In the graphs we saw in the previous chapter, all the nodes had a cost of 1, so the cost of a path would be equal to the number of nodes in the path.

While in an unweighted graph we consider the shortest path the path that has less nodes, in a weighted graph we prefer a path that has the smallest cost – even if it contains more nodes.

The cost in a weighted graph has a semantic related to the space for which the graph is a mathematical model.

The logic behind adding a cost to every node is the same that we would use in everyday life in situations where we have to decide between different ways with different lengths that require a different kind of effort, like for example deciding between a shorter way that requires more effort and a longer way that requires less effort. The effort required to follow a path becomes an added cost that sums up to the length of the path itself. Considering this sum allows us to understand the actual overall convenience of a path.

Figure 4-3. *A pathfinding algorithm that doesn't take into account the costs of climbing 50 m of rocky wall compared to those of walking 500 m on a comfortable path, might take the wrong decision judging which of the two paths is the best*

For example, imagine being in a mountain place and you want to get to the top of a hill to enjoy the view (Figure 4-3). There are two ways to get there: climbing a rocky wall for 50 meters or walking on a 500-meter-long path. There are high probabilities that you will more likely prefer walking on the path because it requires less effort, making it the best and possibly shortest (and safer) way to get there even if the path itself is actually ten times longer. We can say that climbing 1 meter has a much higher cost than walking 1 meter, making the 50 meters climbing less appealing (Figure 4-4).

Figure 4-4. *Adding the cost in terms of effort required to follow the two paths totally changes the situation*

Unity implements weighted graphs for navigation using a solution that's widely appreciated and used in the game industry: the Navigation Mesh. Let's see what it's all about!

4.2 Navigation Mesh

A Navigation Mesh (or NavMesh) is a collection of convex polygons that mark the walkable areas on surfaces in a 3D space. Much like WayPoints, NavMeshes are represented internally as graphs so that graph algorithms can be used to solve pathfinding problems.

While WayPoints are very precise points in the space, a NavMesh is a collection of areas in the 3D space (convex polygons). This difference makes the NavMesh a better solution for smoother and more natural movements.

Using a very user-friendly interface, you can bake (as in generate) a NavMesh in Unity to mark the walkable areas on that surface for a predefined agent. Let's see how this works.

Open up Unity and create a new 3D project. In the main scene, create a GameObject and call it Level. This will be the container for the (very simple) level we are going to create out of primitives.

Create a platform out of a cube with the properties set as in Figure 4-5. This will be the ground of our level.

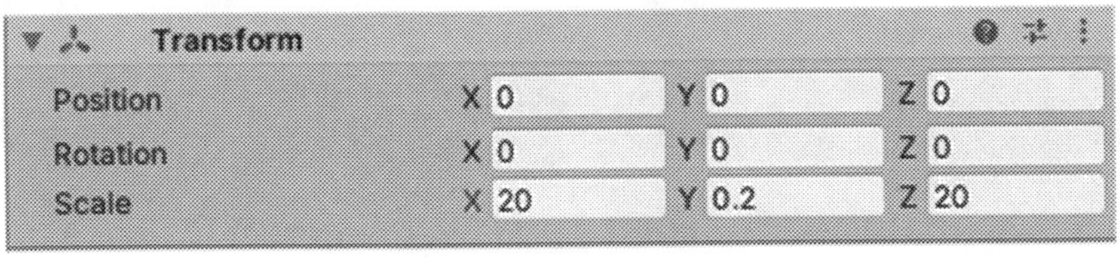

▼ 丄 **Transform**				❷ ⇄ ⁝
Position	X 0	Y 0	Z 0	
Rotation	X 0	Y 0	Z 0	
Scale	X 20	Y 0.2	Z 20	

Figure 4-5. *The properties of the platform that is going to represent the floor*

Now let's create some walls and obstacles on that surface. Create a bunch of cubes and shape and move them to make some walls on our platform. Once you finish, you will end up with something like Figure 4-6 (hopefully better!).

You can add as many 3D objects you want to the level and apply different materials to the objects to define the different parts of the scene, as I did in Figure 4-6. When you finished making it, just drag all those objects into the Level GameObject.

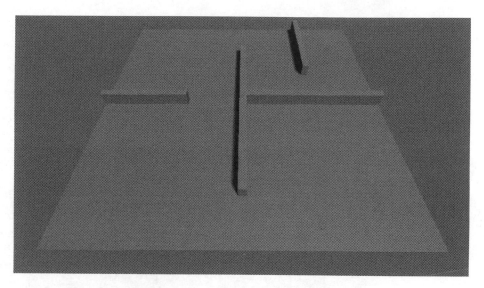

Figure 4-6. *An example of a very simple map*

Now select the Level GameObject, and in the Inspector, click the
Static setting, just next to the textbox containing the name of the object,
and a drop-down menu will open up; from that drop-down menu, select
the setting **Navigation Static**. This will tell Unity to consider the Level
GameObject and all its children as static objects, part of the navigable 3D
space. The consequence of this setting is that, when a NavMesh will be
baked, Unity will consider all the 3D objects marked as Navigation Static
and decide if they are walkable or reachable in any way based on the
characteristics of the predefined agent which we still haven't set up... Let's
do it now!

To open the Navigation panel, you need to go to the Window menu on
the top and select AI ➤ Navigation as shown in Figure 4-7.

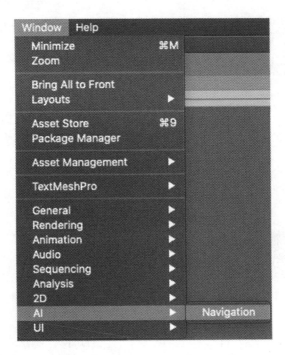

Figure 4-7. How to access the Navigation panel

The Navigation panel will look like Figure 4-8.

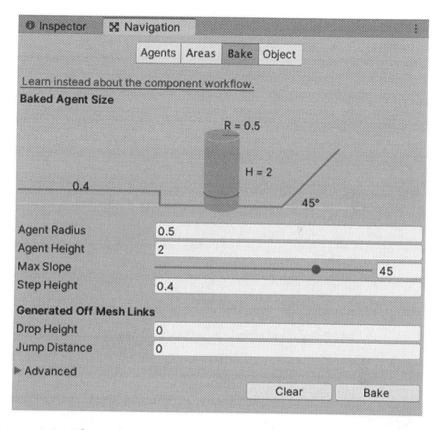

Figure 4-8. *The Bake section of the Navigation panel*

Figure 4-8 shows the Bake section of the Navigation panel. This is the section where you can customize some settings related to the agent. Let's see them in more detail:

- **Agent Radius**: Defines the width of the areas that the agent can walk through (the distance between the walls)

- **Agent Height**: Defines the height of the places that the agent can walk through

- **Max Slope**: The maximum slope that the agent can walk up

- **Step Height**: The maximum height of the steps that the agent can climb

Right after there are the settings related to off-mesh links. Off-mesh links connect meshes that are separated for any reason. It may be because there is a gap between two surfaces or may be because there is a step higher than the Step Height set in the previous section. Off-mesh links, when generated, connect those meshes based on the following settings:

- **Drop Height**: Maximum agent's drop height – if a platform has a drop height higher than this, an off-mesh cannot be generated.

- **Jump Distance**: Maximum agent's jump distance – if two platforms are separated by a distance greater than this, they cannot be linked with an off-mesh link.

If you click Bake, Unity will generate a Navigation Mesh for all the areas marked as Navigation Static based on those settings. Let's do this and you should have something similar to Figure 4-9.

Figure 4-9. *The baked Navigation Mesh for the scene we just created*

Figure 4-9 shows a Navigation Mesh for the geometry created in
Figure 4-6. The blue area is walkable. There are no off-mesh links because
the whole level is pretty simple, and there are no other kinds of areas; they
can be defined in the Area section of the Navigation panel. There you can
also set different costs to different areas as shown in Figure 4-10.

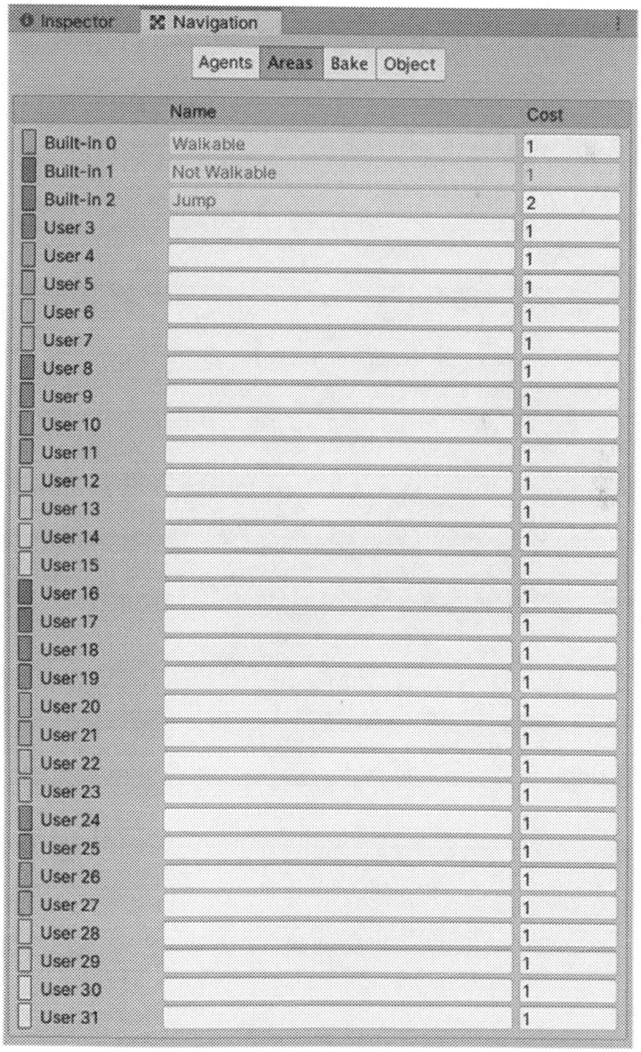

Figure 4-10. *The Areas tab in the Navigation panel allows you to
create different types of areas and assign different costs to them*

Different areas with different costs can lead agents to avoid or prefer some paths instead of others. It's also possible to specify which areas are walkable for an agent so that you can prevent some agents from moving to some specific areas or using them to reach their goal. This feature can introduce a whole lot of possibilities to force agents toward specific paths.

To specify which areas are walkable for an agent, select your agent, and in the Inspector, look for the Area Mask drop-down; by clicking it, you can check which areas you want your agent to be able to walk (Figure 4-11).

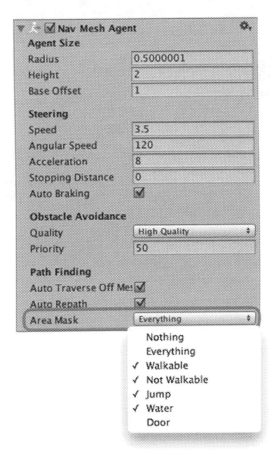

Figure 4-11. *In the Area Mask field, you can specify which area should be walkable for your agent*

Let's try to add some off-mesh links to our map! Pick one of the walls and increase its width to let's say a value of 2, and with that object selected, open up the *Object* section of the Navigation panel; there, check the *Generate OffMeshLinks* box as shown in Figure 4-12 and leave the Navigation Area marked as Walkable. This will make sure that Unity will try to make this object walkable according to the agent's settings and will possibly link it to the floor mesh.

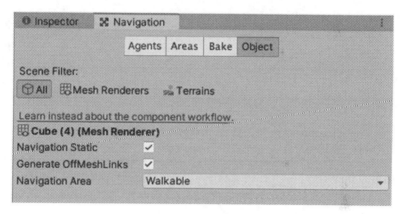

Figure 4-12. *The option to activate off-mesh links for a 3D object is in the Object section of the Navigation panel*

Now that all is set, go back to the Bake section and set Drop Height and Jump Distance to 1 as shown in Figure 4-13 and then press Bake.

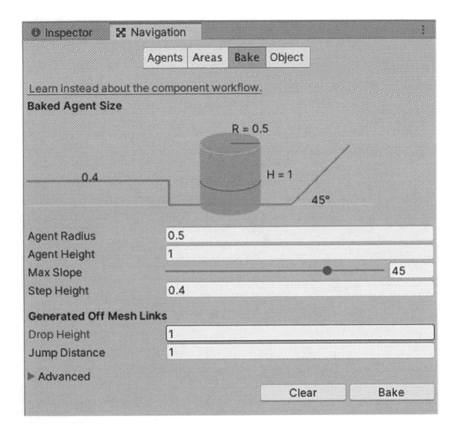

Figure 4-13. *The NavMesh settings updated with the new values for Drop Height and Jump Distance*

The new NavMesh will be baked according to the settings generating a walkable path on the top of the modified wall and connecting that area to the floor using off-mesh links (Figure 4-14).

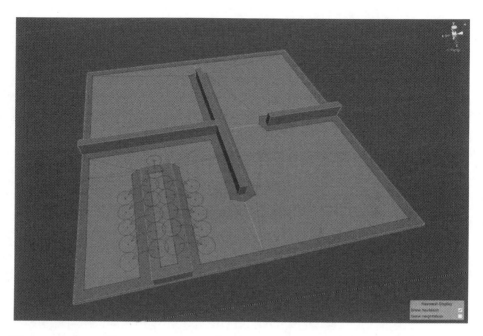

Figure 4-14. *The new NavMesh also contains off-mesh links*

The new NavMesh allows the agent to walk around the map and jump onto the wide-enough wall. The agent will now be able to navigate through the level considering the different costs and taking the best decisions to walk the shortest path toward a specified goal position on the map.

But how can we program such an agent in Unity? And more in general, how does pathfinding work in a weighted system like this?

We need a class of search algorithms that explores a graph taking into consideration the different costs of nodes by expanding them, prioritizing the most convenient ones. These kinds of search algorithms are known as best-first search. Let's take a closer look!

4.3 A Star for Navigation

A best-first search algorithm is a search algorithm that explores a graph prioritizing the most promising nodes. The convenience to expand or not a node is measured by a heuristic function that allows the algorithm to organize the nodes in a priority queue, suggesting the order in which they should be expanded.

A heuristic in problem solving is a practical approach that doesn't promise to be optimal, but it's quick and good enough to achieve a short-term goal or to find a satisfactory solution to a problem.

In the case of best-first search algorithms, a heuristic serves the purpose of finding a node-expansion strategy that's likely to lead to the shortest path by evaluating nodes as they come.

For a real-life example of what a heuristic is and to fully understand its power, think about a scenario in which you're trying to decide the shortest path to get to a shop and there are two ways: one that goes around the buildings and connects you to the front entrance of the shop and one small straight way that passes through a bunch of houses and gets you to the back of the shop (Figure 4-15). Even without measuring the length of the two paths, your brain immediately evaluates both of them and suggests to you that the small straight way is more likely to be the shortest one, as it's a straight way that directly connects you to the shop. Your brain just applied a heuristic assigning an approximative cost to the two paths based on past experience and its ability to perceive the surroundings.

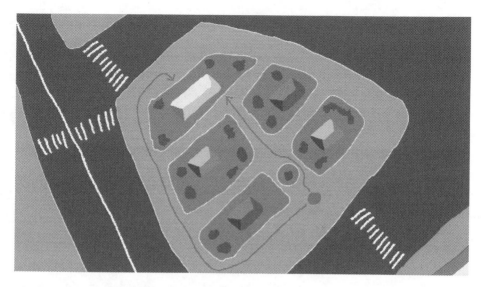

Figure 4-15. *When considering different ways to get to a goal, your brain instictively applies heuristics based on past experiences and knowledge to estimate the overall best path*

The most famous algorithm of that kind is A* (pronounced as A-star), and it's also the de facto standard in solving complex pathfinding problems (especially in 3D spaces) in video games, and this is the reason why it's fully supported inside Unity.

A* uses a very familiar heuristic that we are accustomed to use very often while navigating. It makes a rough estimation of the distance at which the goal might be, not considering the obstacles. We call this the distance as the crow flies; in Computer Science, this is called Manhattan distance.

The A* algorithm assigns to each node a score F = G + H, where

- **G** is the cost to get to the current node from the starting one.

- **H** is the Manhattan distance between the current node and the goal.

Every time the A* agent expands a node, it assigns an F score to all the surrounding nodes and moves to the one with the lowest score.

109

This method allows the agent to get to the goal quickly without suffering Breadth-First Search's side effect of being forced to expand every single node in the graph.

It is clear that A* provides much better overall performances. It's also important to note that the efficiency and in particular the time complexity of A* depend heavily on the heuristics used. A good heuristic will give you a good degree of efficiency, while a bad one might invalidate the algorithm completely.

4.4 Programming Agents

We finally have all the elements to program an agent that can find a path toward a goal point using A* on a weighted NavMesh. It's extremely easy to do in Unity, and we don't even need to implement A* from scratch!

Create a cube in the scene by right-clicking the Hierarchy and selecting 3D object ➤ Cube. Let's call the new object *Agent*. Feel free to apply a material to the object to make it stand out from the rest of the scene.

Unity must be informed that the object we just created is actually an agent for the Navigation Mesh we just created. We can do this by adding a NavMesh Agent component to the Agent object. Select the Agent object, go to the Inspector, and click Add Component; there, look for the NavMesh Agent component and add it to the object.

In Figure 4-16, you can see what the NavMesh Agent component looks like.

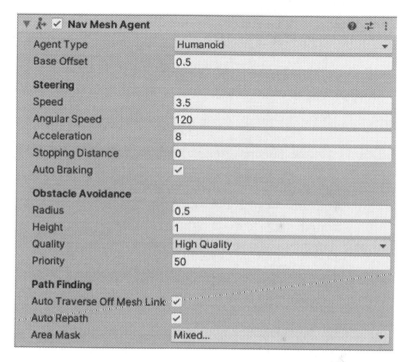

Figure 4-16. *The NavMesh Agent component allows you to personalize the agent*

There you can customize all the settings related to the agent. Let's have a closer look at them:

- **Agent Type**: The type of this agent. Agent types can be defined in the Agents section of the Navigation panel – anyway, since you can only define a single Navigation Mesh based on a single type of agent, you may want to stick with just one type of agent.

- **Base Offset**: The relative vertical displacement of the object.

Following there are all the settings related to steering. We covered steering in detail in Chapter 2. If you think you need to refresh those ideas, go back and have a quick read before continuing reading.

- **Speed**: The navigation speed of the agent.

- **Angular Speed**: The rotation speed of the agent.

- **Acceleration**: The maximum acceleration value of the agent.

- **Stopping Distance**: The distance that the agent will keep from the goal after reaching it.

- **Auto Braking**: Auto-braking allows the agent to stop to avoid overshooting the destination point (because of a high navigation speed).

Following the steering settings, there are the obstacle avoidance settings:

- **Radius**: The obstacle avoidance radius of the agent.

- **Height**: The obstacle avoidance height of the agent.

- **Quality**: This lets you trade between avoidance precision and performance – in fact, calculating the avoidance distances might require some heavy processor workload, depending on the situation and on the quality level set here.

- **Priority**: The avoidance priority of the agent. When the agent is performing avoidance, agents of lower priority are ignored.

Finally, there are some pathfinding-specific settings:

- **Auto Traverse Off Mesh Link**: Should the agent automatically traverse off-mesh links or not?

- **Auto Repath**: Should the agent calculate another path if the current path becomes invalid?

- **Area Mask**: Specifies what kinds of areas are passable for this agent (multiple choice possible).

Now that we have all in place, we just need to add some very basic functionality to allow the agent to move when we select a destination.

Let's create a new C# script with the name AgentController.cs. The script will contain the following code:

```
1.   using System.Collections;
2.   using System.Collections.Generic;
3.   using UnityEngine;
4.
5.   public class AgentController : MonoBehaviour
6.   {
7.       void Update()
8.       {
9.           if(Input.GetMouseButtonDown(0))
10.          {
11.              RaycastHit hit;
12.              if (Physics.Raycast(Camera.main.
                 ScreenPointToRay(Input.mousePosition), out
                 hit, 100))
13.              {
14.                  this.GetComponent<UnityEngine.
                     AI.NavMeshAgent>().SetDestination(hit.point);
15.              }
16.          }
17.      }
18.  }
```

Just as we saw in previous chapters, in **lines 9–12**, we are casting a ray toward the point on the map on which we clicked so that we can have a position in the 3D space to set the goal of the agent. **Line 14** is where the magic happens: with that single line, we are telling the NavMesh Agent component to set the agent's goal to the position on which we clicked. This will make the agent calculate the best path to get to the objective position using the Navigation Mesh we just baked.

That's it; we don't need any other feature, no steering behaviors, no pathfinding implementations: Unity has already everything implemented and set. But it's important to have clear how they work under the hood!

Save the script, attach it to the Agent object, and run the game.

Running the game (Figure 4-17), you will see that clicking any point in the level will make the agent walk toward that point following the shortest path thanks to the A* algorithm working in the background on the weighted NavMesh we just baked!

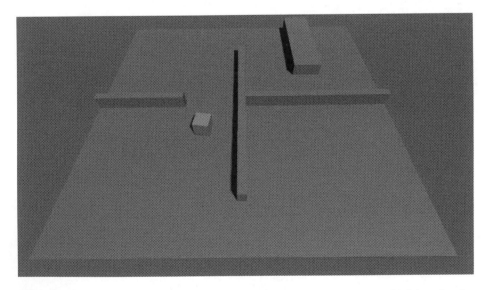

Figure 4-17. *The agent walks toward any point we are clicking in the map*

In this chapter, we saw how easy it is to solve navigation problems in a 3D environment using two powerful tools provided by Unity: Navigation Mesh and A*.

In the next chapter, we are going to do the next step and add behaviors to our agent. We will create a mini stealth game where you must avoid a patrolling guard that is looking for you. We will explore and implement many interesting ideas like a visual cone to allow the guard to perceive the player and a very rudimentary noise system to attract the nearby guard and force them to investigate the location where the sound was coming.

4.5 Test Your Knowledge

1. What is a weighted graph?

2. What is a Navigation Mesh?

3. What's the difference between WayPoints and a NavMesh?

4. What makes a NavMesh better than a WayPoints system?

5. How can you bake a Navigation Mesh in Unity?

6. How can you change NavMesh area costs in Unity?

7. What is A*? How does it work?

8. When is A* convenient?

9. How can you create a NavMesh Agent in Unity?

CHAPTER 5

Behaviors

In this chapter, we are going to further extend our conversation about Game AI taking our first steps towards the creation of believable AI behaviours for the NPCs of our games.

There was a time where video games only had enemies that were moving around without a purpose. The player only had to walk their way past the enemies avoiding their patterns and their bullets and that was the whole threat.

In 1980, Namco changed this trend forever by introducing behaviors for the enemies of a new puzzle game: *Pac-Man*. The enemies in *Pac-Man* were colored ghosts wandering around a maze and occasionally trying to chase the player coordinating their efforts. The incredible thing about *Pac-Man* was that every enemy had a different approach at chasing the player, and it was complementary with the approaches of the other enemies. This made the game feel challenging on a completely new level, because for the first time, the player felt like they were playing against a 'new kind of intelligence,' as Garry Kasparov will describe it in 1997 after his spectacular defeat. Every game felt different from the previous because the enemies were adapting to every new situation and the only way to beat them was to try to outsmart them by trying to predict their approach which, because of the very nature of that new collaborative AI system, wasn't very easy.

The revolutionary AI in *Pac-Man* was based on a series of different *states* in which the enemies could be at any moment in the game, depending on some conditions.

S. M. Cossu, *Beginning Game AI with Unity*,
https://doi.org/10.1007/978-1-4842-6355-6_5

117

Figure 5-1 shows the various states in which *Pac-Man* ghosts can be at any moment. At the start of the game, they spawn and they enter the Roam state and start wandering around the maze. As soon as the ghost sees *Pac-Man*, they enter the Chase state and start to chase *Pac-Man* using their unique strategy. If the ghost loses track of *Pac-Man*, they get back to the Roam state. When *Pac-Man* eats the yellow pill, the ghost enters the Evade state, they become blue and vulnerable to *Pac-Man*, and they start to run away from him.

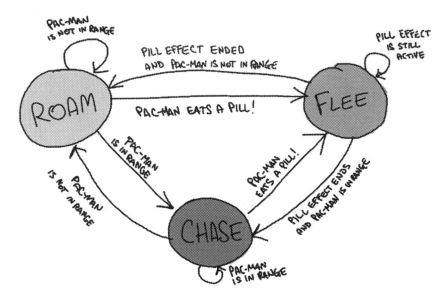

Figure 5-1.   *Pac-Man ghost FSM*

This kind of representation you can see in Figure 5-1 is called Finite-State Machine (FSM).

FSM is a computational model that is used in many different fields (both software and hardware) to design and simulate logic processes. After being crucial in many Computer Science fields, FSM also found their spot in game AI, becoming one of the earliest and easiest (and still used) ways to represent and manage simple AI behaviors.

We will use an FSM to create a behavior for an agent that we will add to the scene we created in Chapter 4. The new agent will patrol the scene wandering around, and it will try to chase the player-controlled character as soon as it will be seen. After the player-controlled character will be out of the cone of sight of the agent, they will go back patrolling the area.

Now that we have a plan, pick up the project we made in Chapter 4, and let's work further on it!

5.1 Guards! Guards!

Let's start by creating a new Game Object that will represent our guard agent in the scene. Create a cube by right-clicking the Hierarchy and selecting 3D Object ➤ Cube.

Rename this new object "Guard" and assign a NavMeshAgent to it by selecting it and clicking Add Component in the Inspector and then Navigation ➤ Nav Mesh Agent. This will allow the new Agent to use the Unity navigation system like the agent we made in Chapter 4.

This new agent will be an autonomous one, capable of reasoning and taking action by itself, so we need to provide it with some **sensors**, to make it perceive the world around it. We are going to give this agent the gift of sight!

5.1.1 Field of View

To give our agent the ability to see, we are going to implement a **field of view** (FOV), which represents the extent of the visible world that is visible at any given moment. Every object inside the field of view can be seen by the agent.

We can translate this concept to C# Unity programming by casting a ray from the agent to the player and checking if the position at which this ray met the player lies inside an area delimited by a certain angle and distance from the agent's position and orientation as shown in Figure 5-2.

Before we start coding, we need to create a tag to assign to the player to make sure that we know we hit the right object.

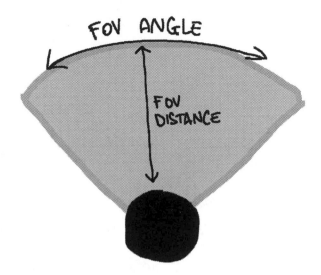

Figure 5-2. *A representation of the FOV that we are going to implement*

Let's do this by selecting the Player object from the Hierarchy, and then in the Inspector, click the Tag field to reveal a drop-down menu from which you can choose or create a new tag. For the purpose of this chapter, we can safely just use the "Player" tag that is already present by default (Figure 5-3).

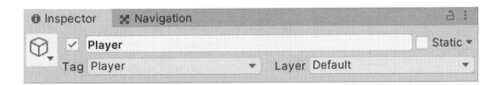

Figure 5-3. *Player tag*

Now, let's create a new C# script with the name "GuardController.cs" and assign it to the Guard agent.

Open the script by double-clicking it and add the following class members on the top of the class definition:

```
1.    public Transform player;
2.    float fovDist = 20.0f;
3.    float fovAngle = 45.0f;
```

The first class member (line 1) is called player, and it represents the player's position. We need to connect the instance of the player's avatar with this member, so that the agent will always be aware of the current position. This is just to easily implement the mechanics, but the agent won't be able to chase the player if they're out of its field of view.

The second and third class members (lines 2–3) represent the depth of the view cone (you can see this as a radius starting from the agent's position) and its wideness represented as an angle in degrees.

As we said, we need to connect the public member *player* to the actual *Player* object. To do that, you need to select the *Guard* object, and then in the Inspector, in the *GuardController* script section, click the player field and select the *Player* object from the list or just drag and drop the *Player* object inside the *player* field.

Now that we have the information about the Player's position, let's define a new method inside GuardController to decide if it can be seen by the Guard's field of view defined by fovDist and fovAngle.

```
1.    bool ICanSee(Transform player)
2.    {
3.        Vector3 direction = player.position - this.transform.
          position;
4.        float angle = Vector3.Angle(direction, this.
          transform.forward);
5.
6.        RaycastHit hit;
7.        if (
```

```
8.              Physics.Raycast(this.transform.position,
                direction, out hit) && // Can I cast a ray from
                my position to the player's position?
9.              hit.collider.gameObject.tag == "Player" && // Did
                the ray hit the player?
10.             direction.magnitude < fovDist && // Is the player
                close enough to be seen?
11.             angle < fovAngle // Is the player in the view cone?
12.             )
13.             {
14.                 return true;
15.             }
16.         return false;
17.     }
```

This method takes a Transform component as a parameter and returns a boolean value. It casts a ray from the current object (this) toward the object passed as a parameter (line 8) and checks if the object hit is tagged as "Player" (line 9) and if it's inside the field of view (lines 10–11). If all the conditions are verified, it means that the object is visible, and so the function returns true (line 14); otherwise, it returns false (line 16).

This code will be used in the Update method of the agent, so that it can *see* at every tick and check if the player is in the view cone and act accordingly.

Let's do a little test by using ICanSee in the Update method, just to see how it works. Modify the Update method like this:

```
1.  void Update()
2.  {
3.      if (ICanSee(player))
4.      {
5.          Debug.Log("I saw the player at " + player.position);
6.      }
```

```
 7.      else
 8.      {
 9.          Debug.Log("All quiet here...");
10.      }
11.  }
```

Now save the script and run the game.

The guard will see anything inside its view cone just in front of it, so just click a point inside its field of view to make the player's avatar walk to that point and allow the guard to notice. You can check the console to verify that the guard is actually seeing the player standing in its field of view.

Now that we have the field of view in place, let's design and code the actual behavior of the agent.

5.1.2 Agents, Behave!

To make our Guard agent act like a proper guard, we need to teach them how an actual guard behaves, so let's design an FSM to describe the behavior we want them to follow.

Tip No matter how easy an FSM can look to you, having a design phase is always a good practice that allows you to get familiar with the flow and also take the opportunity to minimize the FSM where possible.

As we said, we want the guard to patrol the area wandering around randomly. We also want the guard to chase the player as soon as they see them. If the player manages to escape, we want the guard to investigate moving toward the last place they saw the player and then, if the player is not visible, start patrolling again, or chase them otherwise.

This is a kind of FSM that was also used in the classic game *Metal Gear Solid* (Konami, 1998), and it's a pretty good base to understand how a simple behavior can be effective for the gameplay.

From the description of the behavior, we can derive three states:

- **Patrol**: The guard is patrolling the area.

- **Investigate:** The guard is moving toward the last place they saw the player.

- **Chase**: The guard knows the current position of the player and is chasing them.

From the description of the behavior, we can also derive the connections between the states we derived, as shown in Figure 5-4.

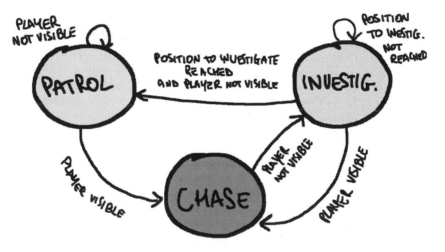

Figure 5-4. *FSM for Chapter 5 agent*

The easiest and most common way to implement an FSM in a programming language is by using an enum to describe the different states that the FSM can get into and check on its current state to execute different pieces of code.

The implementation for our FSM in C# using an enum will look like this:

```
1.    enum State { Patrol, Investigate, Chase };
2.
3.    /* ... */
4.
5.    switch (state)
6.    {
7.        case State.Patrol:
8.            // Patrolling actions
9.            break;
10.     case State.Investigate:
11.         // Investigating actions
12.         break;
13.     case State.Chase:
14.         // Chasing actions
15.         break;
16.   }
```

The previous code will be the skeleton that will allow us to execute the right actions according to the current state. We need to mix this code with the one we already wrote for the field of view, so that we can follow the logic expressed by the FSM in Figure 5-4.

To implement our behavior, first we need some class members that will support the logic and store some important information, so define the following class fields on the top of the definition of the GuardController class:

```
1.    // FSM
2.    enum State { Patrol, Investigate, Chase };
3.    State curState = State.Patrol;
4.
5.    // Player info
```

```
6.    public Transform player;
7.
8.    // Field of View settings
9.    public float fovDist = 20.0f;
10.   public float fovAngle = 45.0f;
11.
12.   // Last place the player was seen
13.   Vector3 lastPlaceSeen;
```

Let's briefly describe them one by one:

Lines 1–2: Here we define the enum that represents all the states of our FSM (line 1) and the State variable that will store the current state in which the agent is.

Line 6: As we already saw, here we define the public member that will be connected to the actual player object so that we can access the player's current position and do our checks for the FOV code.

Lines 9–10: Again, we define here the settings for the FOV, the angle and distance of its view cone.

Line 13: Here, we define a Vector3 variable that will store the information of the last place where we saw the player. We will use this when we will implement the investigate and patrol actions.

Then, modify the Update method inside the GuardController.cs script so that it looks like this:

```
1.    void Update()
2.    {
3.        State tmpstate = curState; // temporary variable to
          check if the state has changed
4.
5.        // -- Field of View logic --
6.        if (ICanSee(player))
7.        {
```

```
8.              curState = State.Chase;
9.              lastPlaceSeen = player.position;
10.        }
11.     else
12.        {
13.            if (curState == State.Chase)
14.            {
15.                curState = State.Investigate;
16.            }
17.        }
18.
19.     // -- State check --
20.      switch (curState)
21.        {
22.            case State.Patrol: // Start patrolling
23.                Patrol();
24.                break;
25.            case State.Investigate:
26.                Investigate()
27.                break;
28.            case State.Chase: // Move towards the player
29.                Chase(player);
30.                break;
31.        }
32.
33.     if (tmpstate != curState)
34.            Debug.Log("Guard's state: " + curState);
35.  }
```

The preceding code contains some placeholder functions (Chase, Investigate, and Patrol) that we will implement in a bit; for now, let's just focus on the general logic of the behavior.

Lines 6–17: We can see the FOV logic being applied to determine the current state. If the guard can see the player, it will chase them (**lines 8–9**); otherwise, if it's currently in a chasing state, it means that the guard just lost track of the player, and so it needs to investigate the point where the player was last seen (**lines 15–16**). We will implement this in the Investigate function by setting the NavMeshAgent goal as the point we want to investigate, and we won't interrupt the investigation until the agent reaches the investigation point.

If the guard cannot see the player, but the current state is different from State.Chase, we don't want to change it, because it means that the guard is patrolling or investigating, so we don't want to disrupt this activity until it's finished or until the guard sees the player.

Lines 21–31: Here, we check all the states and act accordingly. Let's take a closer look:

- **Lines 22–24**: If the guard is in a Patrol state, it just patrols around the lastPlaceSeen point. The patrolling logic inside the Patrol() method will create a new random point to check starting from lastPlaceSeen and set it as a new goal.

- **Lines 25–27**: If the guard is in an Investigate state, we want them to keep investigating. The Investigate method will contain a check that will stop investigating and start patrolling right when the guard will reach the investigation point.

- **Lines 28–30**: Finally, if the guard is in a Chase state, it just keeps chasing the player. The Chase() method will contain the logic to move toward the player if you are not close enough. We will see this in a bit.

Lines 3 and **33–34** are just to log in the console any change of state, so that you can keep track of the Guard's behavior.

OK, now that we have a structure for our behavior, let's implement the three actions that the guard can do.

5.1.3 Chase!

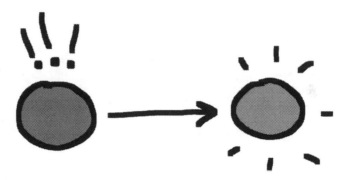

Let's start with the easiest action to implement. What the Chase action does is to just move toward the player's position at a defined speed if the guard is not close enough. We need to use the moving and steering principles we saw in Chapters 2 and 3 to implement this.

We are also going to need three class members to define the walking and rotation speeds and the accuracy, that is basically the space we want to keep between the goal and the agent. Let's add those three class members to the class definition:

```
1.   // Chasing settings
2.   public float chasingSpeed = 2.0f;
3.   public float chasingRotSpeed = 2.0f;
4.   public float chasingAccuracy = 5.0f;
```

Now let's define the actual Chase method:

```
1.   void Chase(Transform player)
2.   {
3.       this.GetComponent<UnityEngine.AI.NavMeshAgent>().Stop();
```

```
4.        this.GetComponent<UnityEngine.AI.NavMeshAgent>().
          ResetPath();
5.
6.        Vector3 direction = player.position - this.transform.
          position;
7.        this.transform.rotation = Quaternion.
          Slerp(this.transform.rotation, Quaternion.
          LookRotation(direction), Time.deltaTime * this.
          chasingRotSpeed);
8.
9.        if (direction.magnitude > this.chasingAccuracy)
10.       {
11.            this.transform.Translate(0, 0, Time.deltaTime *
               this.chasingSpeed);
12.       }
13.    }
```

First, we want to reset the NavMeshAgent component, because when we are chasing, we want the agent to just focus on following the player, and so it needs to forget any patrolling or investigating goal, and we do it by calling the Stop and ResetPath methods of the NavMeshAgent component (**lines 3–4**).

Then, we define the direction we need the guard to look at using the vectors representing the Guard's and player's position (**line 6**), and then we do the actual rotation, so that the Guard can face the Player (**line 7**).

At **lines 9–12**, we check if the Guard is close enough from the player, and if it's not, we want the agent to move forward – thanks to **line 7**, it's the direction where the Player is.

That's all we need to do for the Chase method.

Let's see the next in the line: Investigate!

5.1.4 Investigate!

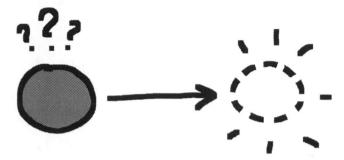

The Investigate method is another simple one. It's derived from what we learned in Chapter 4 about NavMeshes and A*, and thanks to the Unity features, in this method we only need to set a goal for the NavMeshAgent component and make sure it never gets overridden until the agent reaches it or they see the player.

We don't need to add any additional class parameters for this method as we are only going to use the already defined lastPlaceSeen and curState.

So this is the code for the Investigate method:

```
1.   void Investigate()
2.   {
3.       // If the agent arrived at the investigating goal,
             they should start patrolling there
4.       if (transform.position == lastPlaceSeen)
5.       {
6.           curState = State.Patrol;
7.       }
8.       else
9.       {
10.          this.GetComponent<UnityEngine.AI.NavMeshAgent>().
             SetDestination(lastPlaceSeen);
```

```
11.             Debug.Log("Guard's state: " + curState + " point
                " + lastPlaceSeen);
12.         }
13.     }
```

As we said, while we are in the `Investigate` state, we want to stop the investigation only if the guard reaches the point we want them to investigate. We check this at **line 4**, and if the point is still out of reach, we set that point as the `NavMeshAgent` destination (**line 10**); otherwise, if the point was reached, we want the guard to start patrolling (**line 6**).

The `Investigate` method is done; now we only need to add the `Patrol` method. Let's see how to do it.

5.1.5 Patrol!

In this method, we want the `Guard` to pick a random location at a defined distance from the last place where the `Player` was seen and go there.

We want the `Guard` to find a new random location to visit every now and then. We don't want this to be too frequent, to avoid jittering and weird behaviors. The feeling we want to give is that the guard is willingly moving toward a precise point in the space just to look around an area and then move toward another one.

First, we need to define some class members for the class `GuardController` that we will use to set up the patrolling and to control the flow:

```
1.    // Patrol settings
2.    public float patrolDistance = 10.0f;
3.    float patrolWait = 5.0f;
4.    float patrolTimePassed = 0;
```

At **line 2**, we define patrolDistance, which is the distance from the lastPlaceSeen point at which we want to generate the random point to walk to.

At **lines 3** and **4**, we define patrolWait and patrolTimePassed. The former represents the amount of time we want the guard to wait before finding a new random place to go to. The latter is the actual amount of time passed from the last random point generation.

After we defined the logic and those settings, the implementation is pretty straightforward:

```
1.    void Patrol()
2.    {
3.        patrolTimePassed += Time.deltaTime;
4.
5.        if (patrolTimePassed > patrolWait)
6.        {
7.            patrolTimePassed = 0; // reset the timer
8.            Vector3 patrollingPoint = lastPlaceSeen;
9.
10.           // Generate a random point on the X,Z axis
                 at 'patrolDistance' distance from the
                 lastPlaceSeen position
11.           patrollingPoint += new Vector3(Random.Range
                 (-patrolDistance, patrolDistance), 0, Random.
                 Range(-patrolDistance, patrolDistance));
12.
13.           // Make the generated point a goal for the agent
14.           this.GetComponent<UnityEngine.AI.NavMeshAgent>().
                 SetDestination(patrollingPoint);
15.       }
16.   }
```

The Update method calls this method every frame in which the guard is in the patrol state, so the first thing we do is to increase the value of the time passed by Time.deltaTime, which is the time passed (in seconds) from the last frame (**line 3**).

After updating the current passed time, we check if we surpassed the amount of time we want the agent to wait before generating a new point to walk to (**line 5**), and if that's the case, we reset the timer (**line 7**) and we generate a random point on the X and Z axes starting from the lastPlaceSeen position (the last place where the Player was seen) in the range of -patrolDistance and +patrolDistance (**lines 8** and **11**). Finally, the new random position is assigned as a new destination for the NavMeshAgent component (**line 14**).

As a finishing touch, we want to initialize patrolTimePassed and lastPlaceSeen so that the first point is generated at the start of the game starting from the current position of the guard. To do this, we need to use the Start method:

```
1.    void Start()
2.    {
3.        patrolTimePassed = patrolWait;
4.        lastPlaceSeen = this.transform.position;
5.    }
```

That's it! It's all ready! Save the script and run the game and observe your very first behavior FSM in action!

Running the game, you will see the guard moving around in random positions starting from its original position, and if the player ends up in its field of view, it will chase them, and as soon as the player manages to escape, it will investigate the last place it saw them and start to patrol from there in case there is no track of the player (Figure 5-5).

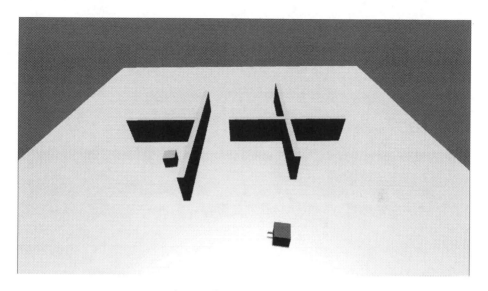

Figure 5-5. *The Player (green) hides from the patrolling Guard (blue) behind a wall*

You probably already understood the power of FSM-driven behavior after seeing the Guard going around patrolling, chasing, and investigating, but to give you a hint of how complex and interesting FSM can get, let's build a little fun feature that leverages what we just created.

5.2 *Knock-Knock* – Who's There?

In the classic stealth game *Metal Gear Solid* (Konami, 1998), you were playing as *Solid Snake*, a spy that had the purpose of infiltrating a secret base and discovering military secrets that were threatening the world! One of the sharpest weapons in *Snake*'s belt was the ability to knock on walls to draw the attention of the patrolling guards and force them to move away from the place they were patrolling to go investigate the position where they heard the noise coming from. This was a crucial ability to master because it allowed you to predict the movements of the guards and free some areas for a small amount of time, allowing you to proceed. We are going to implement this feature in our mini game!

So as we said, additionally to what we already made, we want the possibility to draw the attention of the Guard by knocking. We want this action to force the guard to investigate the current position of the player if the guard is at a certain distance from the player when the knocking happens.

The first thing we need is a method that we can trigger from outside the Guard class, so let's define this additional method inside the GuardController class:

```
1.    public void InvestigatePoint(Vector3 point)
2.    {
3.        lastPlaceSeen = point;
4.        curState = State.Investigate;
5.    }
```

This new method takes a Vector3 as a parameter, which is the position that we want the Guard to investigate. To force the Guard to investigate that point, we just pretend that is the last place where the player was seen (**line 3**), and then we change the Guard's state to Investigate (**line 4**). That's it! In the next iteration, the Guard will start investigating to that new point.

Now, to implement the actual ability to knock on the floor, we want to generate a sphere around the player every time we press the knock key and check the collisions inside this sphere. If the sphere is colliding with a guard, we want to alert that guard and let them investigate the current position of the player using the InvestigatePoint function.

The first thing we need is a tag for our Guard, so that we can recognize it between all the other objects. Just like we did for the player, select the Guard object in the Hierarchy and then go to the Inspector and click the Tag drop-down menu, and this time create a custom tag by clicking Add Tag.... Call the new tag Guard and assign it to the Guard object.

We want the Player to actually make the knocking noise, and to do that, we need to add an AudioSource component to our Player object. Click the Player object in the Hierarchy, and then in the Inspector, click Add Component. Find the AudioSource component from the list and select it to add it to the object. There are many interesting settings to tweak in that component, but we only need to add our audio file, really. So let's click AudioSource's AudioClip field to select our knocking audio file.

Now, let's open up the script associated to the Player object and add this method to be able to play the knocking audio file:

```
1.    IEnumerator PlayKnock()
2.    {
3.        AudioSource audio = GetComponent<AudioSource>();
4.
5.        audio.Play();
6.        yield return new WaitForSeconds(audio.clip.length);
7.    }
```

This is a pretty straightforward code: at **line 3**, we load the AudioSource component, and we play it at **line 5**. **Line 6** makes sure that the routine can be run again only if the audio file has finished playing.

We want to be able to define the strength of the knocking, in case we want to equip our player with different objects or options to make noises of varying strength. So let's define this class member that will define the radius of the collision sphere that is going to trigger the Guard's investigation:

```
1.    public float knockRadius = 20.0f;
```

Finally, in the Update method, add the following code:

```
1.    if (Input.GetKey("space"))
2.    {
3.        StartCoroutine(PlayKnock()); // Play audio file
4.
```

```
5.        // Create the sphere collider
6.        Collider[] hitColliders = Physics.
          OverlapSphere(transform.position, knockRadius);
7.        for (int i = 0; i < hitColliders.Length; i++)
          // check the collisions
8.        {
9.            // If it's a guard, trigger the Investigation!
10.           if (hitColliders[i].tag == "guard")
11.           {
12.               hitColliders[i].GetComponent
                  <GuardController>().InvestigatePoint
                  (this.transform.position);
13.           }
14.       }
15.   }
```

As we said, when the knock key is pressed (**line 1**), we play the sound file (**line 3**), and we create a sphere collider of radius knockRadius (**line 6**); then for every object that collided with our sphere (**line 7**), we check if it's tagged as a Guard (**line 10**), in which case we want to trigger an investigation toward our current position (**line 12**).

Save the script and run the game!

You now have the ability to deceive the Guard forcing them to investigate a point to make them move away from a place. Just like the legendary *Solid Snake*!

In this chapter, you discovered the power of expression that you can achieve with FSM-driven behaviors to teach an agent how to behave intelligently (or apparently so) doing different actions according to the different situations in which they are. The ability to face different situations in different ways is a big part of the concept of rational intelligence.

Even if FSM-driven behaviors are the very first behavior systems used in video games, they are still widely used in many video game genres, and this is because of the efficiency of this method, which is extremely light and powerful, giving great results with very little computational and programming effort.

5.3 Goodbye, AI

In these five chapters, we discovered and addressed many game AI principles, starting from the definitions of AI and agents, passing through pathfinding and search algorithms, and finally ending up creating a small stealth game with an autonomous agent able to patrol, chase, and investigate weird noises and intruders. That was quite a journey!

AI is a very extensive and complex field, and it's always evolving. I hope that this little book managed to give you a good and clear introduction to the foundations of game AI development and will help you in your career as a gameplay/AI developer to improve your skills and build interesting and fun games featuring intelligent (or apparently so) NPCs!

Good luck, have fun!

Index

A

Accuracy, 46
Agent types, 111
Artificial Intelligence (AI)
    intelligent agents, 2, 4
    NPC, 1
    video games, 4–7
AudioSource component, 137
Auto-braking, 112

B, C

Base Offset, 111
Behavior
    class members, 129
    FSM, 125, 126
    states, 124
    Update method, 126, 128
Breadth-First Search
    (BFS), 94, 108, 110
    Agent, 90
    currentNode, 88
    definition, 82
    FIFO data structure, 85
    graph, 83
    implementation, 85
    Update method, 88, 89

D, E

Depth-First Search
    (DFS), 91

F

Field of view (FOV), 119
Finite-State Machine
    (FSM), 5, 118

G, H

Geometric translation, 43
Graphs, 53–56
Graph searching
    algorithms, 57
Guard agent, 123
GuardController class, 136

I, J, K, L

Investigate method, 131, 132
InvestigatePoint function, 136

M

Movement vector, 43

Printed in the United States
By Bookmasters